The Bull Inside the Bear

Finding New Investment Opportunities in Today's Fast-Changing Financial Markets

Robert Stein

WILEY

John Wiley & Sons, Inc.

Published by John Wiley & Sons, Inc., Hoboken, New Jersey.

Published simultaneously in Canada.

For general information on our other products and services or for technical support, please contact our Customer Care Department within the United States at (800) 762-2974, outside the United States at (317) 572-3993, or fax (317) 572-4002.

Wiley also publishes its books in a variety of electronic formats. Some content that appears in print may not be available in electronic books. For more information about Wiley products, visit our web site at www.wiley.com.

Library of Congress Cataloging-in-Publication Data:

ISBN-13 978-0-470-40220-7

Printed in the United States of America

10 9 8 7 6 5 4 3 2 1

To my wife, Eileen, and my son, Spencer, who help me to realize that the most important cycles are life cycles that revolve around family.

Contents

Contents   vii

Foreword

"I watch the economy." It seemed so old-fashioned when I first heard that from Rob Stein. Understand that it was mid-2000 and buying Internet stocks based upon page views was still passing as fundamental analysis. Watching the economy to make investment decisions seemed so behind the times. Wasn't the market supposed to anticipate the economy and forecast trends before they showed up in the statistics? While others were basing strategies on bandwidth capacity, poring over economic data seemed such a quaint and sluggish method to make investment decisions. Though we didn't know it at the time, that was the beginning of a bear market and that was my introduction to Rob Stein.

What Rob knew then was that the economy leads the way. Everything else is noise. Without employment, there are no paychecks. Without paychecks, bills don't get paid. When bills don't get paid, confidence drops. When confidence drops, credit gets curtailed. Or it happens in reverse like it did in 2008. Watching a company's profit margins or a stock chart's trajectory may be telling but it risks mistaking one tree for a forest.

The financial storm that overtook the world in late 2008 can trace its beginnings back to many sources. But just as many investors limit their focus, so too did regulators. Growing revenues may be wonderful until an investor realizes the company is self-financing customer purchases with easy terms in order to make its current quarterly projections. Or how about that giant debt payment coming due with little hope of refinancing it and few assets left to sell to raise cash? Myopic financial regulators (and investors) got caught off-guard and unprepared for the massive amounts of securitized leverage that had been built up because no one had a complete picture. Not only had Americans borrowed more than they could really afford but those IOUs had been bought and sold with no regard for the ability to actually repay the debt. In the process of spreading the risk around, the mechanism to measure the fundamental risk was compromised.

No one was watching the entire "economic" portfolio. Investors are angry and scared, and for good reason. They want to know who is to blame. They want to know who is going to jail. Every horror story needs a villain to despise, but the villain here may be our own appetite to consume with little regard for what Rob focuses on: cycles. Sure, it was easy to borrow loads of cash to fill our homes with big TVs and stainless steel appliances. We had to buy two-and-a-half car garages to fit our two big SUVs. Companies were too willing to "make the numbers work" and the market rules were too outdated to watch over the new avenues of credit. We borrowed until we couldn't anymore. The cycle turned and despite plenty of warning signs, it rolled over with devastating results for millions of Americans, homeowners, and investors.

The slapdash government response, however necessary, in late 2008 was just as unsettling as the financial storm itself. Attaching a problem is impossible without clear agreement on what the problem is, but is there time for definition when default is threatened? Perhaps not. This adds to investors' anxiety and anticipation. How bad will it be and when will it end?

Those same questions were asked in 1990 and 1981 and certainly in 1931. Through 10 economic cycles in the last half of the twentieth century, the average recession lasted 10 months. The average time between the bottom of economic cycles was five-and-a-half years and the upswings lasted about five-and-a-half years, according to the National Bureau of Economic Research. This data includes the post-war boom during the industrial age, the energy crisis of the 1970s, double digit inflation of the early 1980s, and the transformation into the Information Age by the turn of the century. We've seen about two boom and bust cycles every decade, dating back to 1945.

Going back almost 150 years, economic cycles have averaged even shorter life spans, only four-and-a-half years. It's difficult to forget our most recent cycles, though. The 2001 recession was among the shortest and shallowest in history. And that almost one-dimensional drop came on the heels of the longest expansion on the books. These were not typical, and neither is the cycle that turned in 2008.

Each shrinking economy has been able to pull itself together and growth has been reignited for different reasons, both universal and particular to the times. Confidence returns, hiring rebounds and new opportunities are found. Preparing for those opportunities demands patience, persistence, and an appreciation for context.

In each cycle, there will be someone who claims, "This time, it is different." The New Economy played by different rules in the late 1990s. Actual profits weren't as important as the growing potential for profits. In the 1970s, peak oil was going to mean the end to petroleum as a viable energy source. The new sources of credit earlier this decade made old lending standards obsolete and those old standards obstructed profits, but in each case, fundamentals did eventually matter again. The economy used energy more efficiently. Real profits mattered. Standards were restored.

The return to fundamentals isn't painless but it is necessary to sow the seeds of the next boom.

Tom Hudson
Managing Editor
First Business TV
Chicago, IL
November 2008

Preface

I was asked to write this book during one of the most "unique" periods in economic history—and I use that word intentionally. When we get beyond the other words like "meltdown" and "crisis" and "panic" and "bailout," we see that 2008 has been a time like no other, comparable only to the Great Depression. (And as bad as it is, it's not even close.)

As of this writing in late 2008, nothing in my personal experience can compare with the current conditions: not the double-digit inflation period of the late 1970s or the double-dip recession of the early 1980s; not the stock market crash of the late 1980s or the savings and loans crisis and the mild—but election-determining—recession of the early 1990s. I traded and invested through the Russian debt crisis and currency devaluation of the late 1990s; the bust of the NASDAQ and the recession and bear market of the post-9/11 2000s. So I do have some perspective when it comes to labeling this time unique.

However, I do believe that this time—no matter how tumultuous—will be like each of these previous pivotal economic events. What followed them was an expansion or bull market—not always in stocks, but in some investable asset. Following every economic catastrophe to date, one sector or another has come alive, thereby proving that the end of the world was not upon us and the sky did not fall. Opportunity presented itself, if you just knew where to look.

The same, I believe, will occur when the financial crisis of 2007 and 2008 is finally behind us, and quite possibly before. Once again, you will need to know where to look and how to capitalize upon opportunity. That's where this book comes in, with discussion of the housing bubble, the credit crisis, and recent Fed policy. More importantly, I hope to educate readers about how to look at economic fundamentals and determine how and where to make their investment decisions.

This is not a book for market timers or traders who want to profit from every little zig and zag that the market and economy make. It is to evaluate cycles and long-term trends that will make you a more productive and efficient investor. Or at the very least you will understand why long-term fundamentals determine the direction of an asset class or the overall market.

In my first book, *Inside Greenspan's Briefcase,* I stated that buy and hold doesn't work. Sure, it worked for a few decades and, statistically speaking, stocks are positively sloped over a long period of time. But if you look at a more realistic measure of risk and return, buying and holding through every cycle of expansion and contraction doesn't make sense. Take the average long-term return on stocks and you will get a range of 7 to 10 percent (depending on start and end date, dividends, etc.). Even disregarding a long-term average inflation rate of, say, 3 percent, the result is a very lopsided risk/return profile: risk 50 to 70 percent for an average 8 percent annual return. Does that make sense?

As investors I think we need to change the risk/return profile first by acknowledging that we are already accepting more risk than we realize. And if so, we should change our investment goals to improve the potential for the overall return. What we learned and experienced earlier in the decade is that stocks can have large declines and that portfolios, if not properly diversified, can suffer. The two-year decline from 2000 to 2002 was the largest decline ever since the Depression and a mere six years later we saw it happen all over again.

Timing is not the answer as I don't think you can time entry and exit points with enough accuracy to make it a productive strategy. One wrong step and the entire strategy will be for naught. However, as you will learn from *The Bull Inside the Bear,* there are fundamental conditions that are advantageous for stocks—and these fundamentals exist in many different sectors. While this may sound like market timing it is not. It's predicated on economic cycles.

As you'll read throughout this book, I am a strong believer in recurring cycles, which can be identified quite accurately with observations. To draw a comparison, even if you didn't know the exact date winter begins (actually it's December 21), you would certainly know when it starts to get cold and stay cold in December. One cold day in October isn't enough to get you thinking that it's winter. Economic fundamentals are similar: sometimes it's just a number (like a cold day is just a cold day) and sometimes a string of numbers in a row indicates a significant shift into a new "season."

By watching the economic climate conditions, you will learn when to reduce exposure to the market as a whole, as well as to change your exposure within individual sectors or asset classes. You will identify correlations with the overall market and truly diversify your portfolio. Additionally, you will learn why individual stocks may not be the best way to create a bulletproof portfolio and why the increasingly popular exchange-traded funds (ETFs) may very well be the best thing to ever happen to your portfolio.

Buy and hold was *so* twentieth century. Now it's time to get with the times, with tools and information that you can use to create a diversified portfolio. This will allow you to insulate your portfolio from adverse major market moves, while positioning you to take advantage of structural economic changes.

At my firm, Astor Asset Management, LLC, we use this same approach to analyze and interpret economic data to form the basis of our investment opinion for the overall market, as well as for specific sectors. We also seek to identify those sectors that are likely to perform best, based on the prevailing economic trend. To do that, we study economic data to determine what's going on *right now*. Is the economy gaining or losing jobs overall? Is one particular sector adding jobs? Is another experiencing an employment decline? Do we have wage inflation? Is GDP growing or shrinking and at what rate? These analyses give us insight into the current phase of the economy. Additionally, these data points are consistent within specific asset classes as well as the overall economy.

Of course these data points may be lagging and catching the top or bottom of the market is unlikely. Again this is not a market-timing approach. However, history has proven that investing in the direction of the prevailing trend will reap better rewards than timing. Sure you might be late, but as the old saying goes, "better late than never." And from where I sit I have seen a lot of never. For example, if you waited out the recession of 1991 and 1992 and didn't feel comfortable or confident enough to get back into the overall market until 1995, you still would have doubled your investment during the expansion. Further, when the contraction hit in late 2000, if you held on mid-2001—a full year after the peak—to get out, you still saved yourself 30 to 40 percent. As you know, you would need almost a double to get back to even. This is an example of getting the direction right but not necessarily the exact time.

As we know, the economy moves in cycles: expansion, peak, contraction, and trough. At any given moment, it's easier to determine which of these four very distinct cycles the economy is in than it is to forecast precisely when the next one is coming. Once we identify the current stage of the economy, we invest accordingly.

We focus on the economy because we believe it is everything—the engine that generates growth and drives wealth for consumers and businesses alike. This is the basic premise of our philosophy at Astor Asset Management, as explained in my last book. We believe the best way to access or get exposure to an asset class that has an identifiable trend is through ETFs. To that end, we have created a web site—www.etfport.com—to aggregate the fundamental data needed to evaluate ETFs, sectors, and the economy, and to help investors make decisions.

In *The Bull Inside the Bear,* I will drill deeper into economic expansions, look at why they burst, discuss how to identify bubbles, and explore the recent credit bubble and its implication on investments going forward. I will also discuss how your investment toolkit will be further fortified by the emergence of ETFs that represent virtually every conceivable index, sector, and subsector of the economy. Want exposure to energy, chemicals, retail, or restaurants? How about mid-cap, small-cap, large-cap, or companies with a certain capitalization in a specific part of the world? There's an ETF that you can buy to gain that exposure. The proliferation of ETFs makes it easier for you to gain exposure to specific sectors, instead of having to cherry pick among the countless company names and stock recommendations out there, hoping to find the next Google.

As I see it, the stock market will be the place for investor wealth in the years ahead now that the torch has passed. Real estate has had its run, and now it's time for stocks to begin the race. We'll know the starting gun has sounded when the economic data points to growth once again, after a recession that is both necessary and healthy: trimming the fat, making companies more efficient, cooling off inflationary forces. Then the stock market will be in for a long, good stretch.

And that's the bull inside the bear.

Rob Stein
Astor Asset Management
www.etfport.com

Acknowledgments

The process of writing a book is particularly satisfying when it is finally complete and you can look back on the experience and all those who supported the effort.

This is my opportunity to thank those individuals who not only tolerated me during the process, but who also contributed to it. As I have matured in life and speed bumps abound, it has become clear that without support a project such as *The Bull Inside the Bear* might never get completed.

As a husband and father I can't express enough thanks for the support of my wife, Eileen, and my son, Spencer, to whom this book is dedicated. While it may have looked like I was using the "deadline excuse" to circumvent other responsibilities, I really did write better when alone in front of the TV watching a Cubs game. Now that the book is finished, I have some family time to catch up on.

Thank also to:

Tricia Crisafulli, who not only inspires me to work harder (and faster) but helps me find my voice. This book could not have been accomplished without her.

To everyone at Astor who picks up my slack when I get buried, especially: Scott Martin, Bryan Novak, and Scott Thomas, who help move the ball forward and work tirelessly on any and all projects that need to be completed. Thanks to Sarah Bancsy who has kept me organized over the past ten years. Thank you, Althea Trevor, who is wise beyond her years and amazes me with the new and innovative ideas she has as she takes my concepts to the next level.

To my editor, Kevin Commins, who from our first conversation helped to shape this book.

Part I

THE CREDIT MARKET MELTDOWN

Chapter 1

How Has the World Changed?

H istory, as they say, repeats itself, and nowhere is this truer, perhaps, than in the economy. We find comfort in the predictability as the economy cycles through the four stages of expansion, peak, contraction, and trough. We tell ourselves that yes, indeed, the more things change the more they stay the same.

The world, however, has changed. This sentiment is evidenced in the level of federal government intervention to bailout, stabilize, and otherwise jumpstart the financial sector—a plan presented at $700 billion, which could balloon even higher. We see it in the government takeover of mortgage giants Freddie Mac and Fannie Mae and in the $100 billion-plus rescue and takeover of insurance company AIG. Being "too big to fail" is a battle cry that has the Treasury Department and the Federal Reserve running for their checkbooks.

"The world has changed," declared a spokesperson for Morgan Stanley, which after 75 years of being an investment firm decided to go back to being a bank—a step also taken by Goldman Sachs (and many others who want access to government money and cheap capital). In the process, they face more regulation, presumably less risk, and probably lower profits in return for consumer saving deposits as a source of funds—as well as access to the Federal Reserve discount window.[1]

The federal government's $700 billion bailout of Wall Street to buy discounted and troubled assets, many of them subprime loans, was supposed to put in a floor to keep the financial sector from spiraling lower, boost investor confidence in financial firms and the stock market in general, and help stabilize the housing market where home values have been declining at a dizzying rate—that is, when properties are sold. In the 11th hour, Treasury Secretary Henry Paulson, citing that conditions had changed, decided to focus on supporting the banking system. He pumped money into financial institutions in hopes of getting credit flowing again. If it works, then sometime in the future the great bailout of 2008 will be one those notable times, like the savings and loan crisis of the 1990s. We'll study it as a classic textbook case of crisis and intervention, and debate the merits of the expansion of the government's actions. If the bailout does not work (and as you'll read in Chapter 4, as a free market advocate I take issue with the extensiveness of the federal government's intervention), then the landscape may look even more different.

In the midst of the crisis, during the summer and fall of 2008, things looked very scary. The situation was referred to as the biggest crisis since the Great Depression. It was bad, and it felt even worse as stocks suffered 5+ percent daily moves regularly, and fears escalated that the next bank to go under would be the one with your paycheck in it. Money market funds were in danger of "breaking the buck" and cash on deposit was feared to be "money gone." The proverbial domino effect was about to fall into place as the system jammed.

Although it was bad, I don't believe we were about to have financial Armageddon. The events of 2008 stemmed from a breakdown in the financial system, not the economy. The economy was already weak and this was a hit where it really hurt. But the economy was still standing. Gross domestic product (GDP) grew by more than 3 percent in the second quarter of 2008 (although this could be revised downward). The preliminary report for third quarter showed a contracting economy with GDP down 0.3 percent. As of October 2008, 94 percent of the workforce was employed. Yes, we were in a contraction, but the economy was far from screeching to a halt. Even if the third quarter is revised lower, as it most likely will be, and the fourth quarter looks dismal because of the largest drop in consumer spending in two decades, the fundamental problem is the financial system—not an economy that was broken. In other words, we're having a garden variety recession on top of a financial crisis.

The financial system had to brake hard, but that was not bringing the economy to its knees. This was far different from the weak economy of 1929 to1932, which in turn, caused a breakdown in the financial system. In 2008, we had the opposite: a breakdown in the financial system that was dragging down an already contracting or slowing economy. This is a vital distinction to understand when surveying the current landscape.

As became apparent by late 2008, there have been fundamental—and most likely permanent—changes to the economy and, by extension, to society. The way we buy a house, make and finance large purchases, invest for the future, and even how and where we work have all been irreversibly altered due to the financial crisis. Buying a house, which in the not-so-distant past could be sparked by a conversation with a mortgage broker and after spotting a for-sale sign somewhere, will become a cautious undertaking. Shopping with a credit card will no longer be second nature; cash will make a comeback. People will probably not hop jobs as frequently because they're thinking twice about employment security.

Central to the theme of this book, investing has forever changed. The financial crisis and the toll taken on Wall Street have proven that buy-and-hold does not work—not with two 50 percent declines in the same decade. Retirees simply do not have enough time to make up for losses with buy-and-hold. Even those who are younger will be scrambling to repair the damage to their 401(k) plans—which makes people long for (and perhaps seek out) jobs with pension plans.

From what I observe, the aftermath of the financial crisis has resulted in a paradigm shift that is more profound than the change in behavior after September 11th. Moreover, as of this writing, the impact and magnitude of these changes are unfolding.

Although there have been fundamental changes in consumer and investor behavior, market forces will continue to hold some sway. We will still see the same cycles. Yes, the credit crisis is unique; but we can still draw lessons from the not-too-distant past to see that we've been in deep contractions before, just as we've gone through expansions. And we'll be there again.

Although my personal experience mostly covers the 1980s, 1990s, and today (which may sound like the promo for an all-hit radio station), for the sake of this discussion I will also include the 1970s, during which my work experience was limited to paper routes and being a vendor and an usher, but still enough to form a prospective. Let's take a look at some of the highlights of each of these decades in broad terms.

- The 1970s: High energy prices, Arab Oil Embargo, double-digit interest rates, Paul Volcker in charge of the Fed
- The 1980s: Stock market "crash" of 1987, interest rates, Alan Greenspan in charge of the Fed, savings & loan crisis, junk bonds, merger & acquisition activity
- The 1990s: Long bull market, Asian credit crisis, Long Term Capital Management, Dot-com revolution, low interest rates, Greenspan at the Fed
- The 2000s: Technology bubble bursts bear market correction, low interest rates, Greenspan era comes to a close, credit crisis, inflation makes a comeback, credit crisis causes a liquidity drain

Looking at these highlights decade-by-decade, we can see that each period is distinct. And certainly no other period of history has been exactly like another decade. I would argue, however, that the distinctions involved are actually quite subtle; the way that no two snowflakes are alike. Although the patterns of crystals may be different, snowflakes are still more like each other than, say, a snowflake and a raindrop. So, too, with periods of history when viewed through an economic lens: There are differences among specific time frames, but often it is only a matter of degree.

So has the world changed? Yes. Has the economy changed? Yes. But the capitalist democracy that our economy enjoys, with recurring cycles of expansion, peak, contraction, and trough, has not changed— even as every financial crisis and downturn portends to be the last one.

With a deeper understanding of the cyclical nature of the economy, and the expansions that create bull markets and the contractions that result in bear markets, we can look to the future for investment opportunities. While an understanding of the past is important, what will benefit you the most as an investor is to know how to apply the lessons gleaned from history. This means looking for the bull market opportunities that emerge as the next expansion occurs in one area, and avoiding the bear markets that occur as another area contracts.

The Next Bull and Bear

For those of you who have to know how the story ends, I will tell you what this book is working up to: the next bull market expansion and also the upcoming bubble burst and contraction. The expansion will be in equities, driven by an increase in corporate profits. The next bubble that bursts will be in Treasury securities. Now, that doesn't mean that you should immediately put down this book and run over to the computer screen or the telephone to buy stocks and sell bonds right now. As you'll read in Part III, there are also specific indicators or triggers that we need to look for in order to confirm that the bull has emerged in a particular market or that the bear has come out of his cave in another.

The bigger point to make here is that even in the midst of a bear market contraction in one area, an opportunity is setting up in another. As of this writing, the aftermath of the credit crisis and the bursting of the housing bubble continue to weigh on the economy and the stock market. While consumers in general and homeowners in particular are wringing their hands over lower housing prices and tighter availability of mortgages and other financing, it's not the end of the world. Rather, as we'll discuss in upcoming chapters, an overexpansion in housing and liquidity created a bubble scenario, which overexpanded and then burst. The bigger the mess, the longer it takes to clean up and return to equilibrium.

But the remedy for a problem in one sector becomes the tonic to boost activity and opportunity in another. The key is to look for the remedy and follow it where it flows. And that, in a nutshell, is the bull inside the bear.

A Valuable History Lesson

The reason we know to look for a new bull market expansion to capitalize upon, or to avoid the next bear market contraction, is that history does, indeed, repeat itself. We can take what we saw (and hopefully learned from) in the past and apply it to the future. Although we can count on the cycles reoccurring, I thought it might be interesting to look deeper into why. Not just from an economic policy standpoint, but also from a social and behavioral view as well.

Changes to interest rates and money supply will have identifiable textbook outcomes. However, when changes in workforce demographics meet changes in wages and money supply growth, the outcome is less predictable. For example, women entering the workforce in the 1970s and 1980s, as never before, changed the labor pool forever. In upcoming chapters, we will explore more deeply this fundamental workforce change and how it impacted the economy, inflation, wages, and so forth.

Technology changes like the personal computer, introduced in droves during the 1980s, was a technological revolution that also impacted everything, including the way we work and conduct business. Even Bill Gates' mother could not understand the impact or the need for a PC on every desk and the impact on the economy. What we have seen in time is that the worker productivity increase from having a PC on every desk created a boom that no one could have predicted based on economic data analysis alone. Once it became clear that businesses of all shapes and sizes could not survive without a computer and the software that powered it, the race was on to maximize its potential. A lull occurred in productivity as the skill set needed to program and in some cases even just to run a simple program was in short supply. Programmers and IT positions commanded higher wages and more sophisticated training.

By the 1990s, the workforce had become more competent with computers, and productivity gains continued. Jobs initially intended for higher skilled workers with computer competency were being done by assistants and first-year new hires to whom computer knowledge was second nature. This shift had profound changes on the workforce as lower-skilled workers, in some cases, had knowledge that higher-paid employees did not. Business could increases their productivity by hiring efficient, sometimes younger, and less expensive employees. While the economy enjoyed employment gains, older, higher paid workers found it more challenging to find satisfactory employment. This shift was the beginning of even greater changes. These workers were more entrepreneurial and less rooted. Moving and quitting a job for another one was factored into where and how they worked. This also gave rise to the younger homeowner.

Workforce changes caused a rethinking of economic data. In fact, after the recession of the early 1990s, Federal Reserve Chairman Alan Greenspan noted a sudden increase in orders for computers, chips, and components, along with the increase in hiring of the computer savvy sect by small and mid-sized businesses. These developments were noted well before the economic data turned, declaring the end of the recession. The technology revolution was now the foundation of business development and growth, and hence led the way for the next expansion. While every other gray-haired economist was looking for production and manufacturing data to turn, the cutting-edge leading indicator was new orders for computer parts and job growth fostered by the small businesses—which account for more than half the private-sector jobs in the United States.

The economy has changed over the years from agriculture to manufacturing to service to financial to information. Each change has brought about new dynamics to analyzing the change in cycles. At the end of the 1990s and the beginning of the next millennium, the development of the Internet changed the way we work and communicate, and also changed the way we live—or should I say where we live. Now, thanks to high-speed Internet and Federal Express, you can work from almost anywhere and at any time. This helped fuel massive development that spawned the ex-burbs and suburban sprawl. Mega-malls and McMansions spread across the land. Twenty-four hours a day you can find a Starbucks, Kinko/FedEx, and Walgreens open and ready for you to work, shop, and play anytime, all the time. It's not just a "city that never sleeps," as Sinatra told us, but apparently the suburbs never take a snooze either.

Business' answer to the migration out of the city was not to build a significant high-rise in any major city other than Chicago and New York for nearly a decade as developments and office parks proliferated on farmland, swampland, and rural open lots. This led to the rise of the soccer mom and the two-car-and-one-SUV family. While commuting for work declined, shuttling the kids to activities increased, as did overall short-mile trips because the new suburbs had few places to which one could walk.

Society changes for good or bad, and my views on these changes are just one man's opinions and, of course, subject to change—just because. But let's take a look at what consumers value and where they put their time, attention, and dollars.

At the turn of the twentieth century, economist and sociologist Thorstein Veblen gave us the leisure class and conspicuous consumption, with consumers more interested in the status-value than the utility of their purchases. The turn of the twenty-first century brought consuming conspicuously to another level, with bigger-is-better for houses, cars, SUVs, and television screens. It makes me wonder what will come next, with the rise of energy consciousness and green (as opposed to greed) being good. Will the next status symbol be the electric car or the bicycle? Will people compare the size of their backyard compost piles or recycling bins? And don't forget we've been here before, in the 1970s when we tried to "save the planet" and "Earth Day" celebrations declared the end of the hydrocarbon-burning engine (obviously, a bit premature). Whatever societal and demographic changes emerge, rest assured they will have an impact on the economy.

New societal developments—combined with fluctuations in inflation, employment, wages, and growth—play a significant role in why cycles change faster or harder, or why a contraction is shallower or shorter than if one viewed the data alone. While it's important to take into account shifts in demographics and spending patterns, and their influence on the economy, it's important not to let one's own opinion color the reality of what is really happening in the economy. For me, the stalwart economic indicator of employment pervades my analysis. Yet I cannot ignore immigration, outsourcing, discrimination, and so forth to make an informed decision on the economy. Opinions on these topics aside, the reality is what we will discuss.

For example, beginning in 2007 and through early 2008, inflation became a concern. Then late in 2008, deflation grabbed our attention as a host of assets, especially commodities, dropped by a third or a half as they were sold to raise cash. In the wake of deflation, we will need an inflationary environment to help restore the value of these assets. Inflation will make a comeback (a task the Fed is particularly good at) and it will most likely be greater than we've seen in the past.

Earlier in 2008, inflation was suddenly staring us in the face with gasoline prices over $4 a gallon and gold approaching $1,000 an ounce. This seemed to be a tremendous difference from the 1990s when inflation appeared to be a nonissue, and much more similar to the late 1970s when inflation was the hot button topic. The Fed may have appeared to put inflation concerns on the back burner for a decade or two in the 1980s and 1990s; however, from a purely economic standpoint, the fact is inflation is *always* an issue. (Even after the deflationary period of late 2008, inflation will become an issue again.) To illustrate, one of the primary functions of the Federal Reserve is to establish U.S. monetary policy to keep inflation under control. It may be that economic conditions at a particular point in time are not inflationary, but that doesn't mean inflation is any less important. And it's not like the Federal Reserve can take extra long holidays because there's no inflation and the Fed governors have nothing to do. Inflation is still on the radar screen; it's just not moving any closer to the target.

Economic events that grab headlines and send gyrations through the markets do color a specific decade a certain way, whether it's high inflation in the 1970s or the dot-com boom of the 1990s. For the decade of the 2000s, the credit crisis is a distinct feature of this time frame. When we take a step back and examine the credit debacle as a bubble that burst, however, we see there are far more similarities between what happened in the 2000s and other events of the recent past. The boom and bust of the credit market is not all that different, for example, from the dot-com explosion and crash and the sharp decline in the stock market that ensued.

As Figures 1.1 through 1.3 show, there have always been bubbles— the hyper-economic expansion of overextension, unrealistic valuations, and irrational exuberance. While markets and time frames involved differ, what remains the same is the economic propensity for creating bubbles.

My premise, therefore, is that, no, the world hasn't really changed. Some of the indicators may have changed and the causes of the cycle changes are different, but the recurring cycles are still with us, time after time. The same issues continue to affect us, but some to a greater degree than others. In some phases, inflation is more of a factor than others. Or, a particular sector or investment opportunity may become

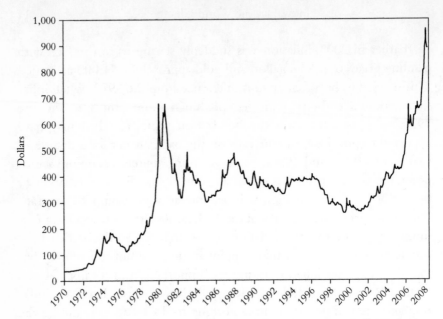

Figure 1.1 A Bubble in Gold in the 1970s Followed by a Long Lull—and Another Spike in 2007 and 2008
SOURCE: http://www.kitco.com.

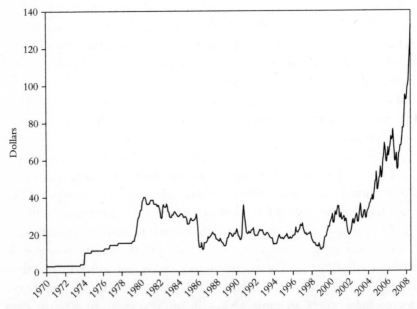

Figure 1.2 The Previous Price Peaks in Oil Pale by Comparison with the "Mount Everest" of Prices in early 2008
SOURCE: Federal Reserve Bank of St. Louis: FRED.

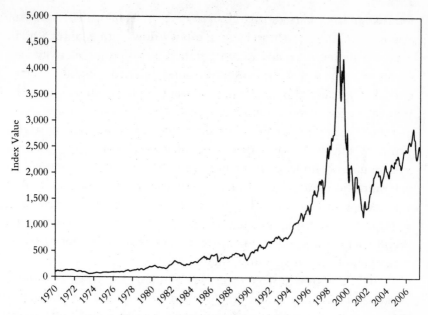

Figure 1.3 NASDAQ Peaked in Late 1999–Early 2000, Fueled by the Tech Stock Bubble
SOURCE: The Nasdaq Stock Market, Inc. (NASDAQ): NASDAQ.com.

overheated. Regardless of the factors that are grabbing the attention in the foreground, the most important things are happening behind the scenes. Here, in the background, the economy continues to cycle through its phases, each identifiable and distinct.

The Four Stages of a Recurring Cycle

The U.S. economy experiences four stages of a recurring cycle, otherwise known as the business cycle: expansion, peak, contraction, and trough. One can determine the current stage of the economic cycle by examining and analyzing economic data, such as GDP, inflation, and unemployment. From an investment perspective, one can make decisions based on the current economic cycle to take advantage, for example, of an expanding economy, or to adopt a more defensive posture during times of contraction.

Here are typical qualities of each of the four phases of the economic cycle.

- Expansion: Characterized by ascending employment growth, positive GDP growth, and strong money flows into equities. Often, an expanding economy is also signified by rising productivity and output, as well as rising consumer confidence and spending.
- Peak: Typically this phase is consistent with "irrational exuberance" in the markets, rampant prosperity, and, in some cases, overbought equity prices. While productivity and output remain strong during this cycle, they show signs of weakness and inconsistency. Consumer confidence also tends to reach a high at these levels.
- Contraction: After the peak comes the contraction. Noticeable weakness in economic data begins to surface, such as: decreasing employment, rising unemployment, leveling-off of productivity, and overall output decreases. Money flows that come out of equities favor fixed income investments and money markets.
- Trough: The trough stage of the economy occurs when economic data, such as output and employment, are at their lowest points. Consumer confidence and spending also hit new lows. Productivity tends to fall as output bottoms and morale decreases. Money flows into equities are at their lowest point, while money market investments are in favor.

Two distinct snapshots in time provide an insightful look at the four stages at work, as the economy cycles from expansion to peak, and then contraction to trough, and back again. Figure 1.4 shows Gross Domestic Product (GDP) during the 1950s. As the chart clearly displays, the economy slowed through 1951 and, after a brief reprieve in mid-1952, declined sharply through 1953 into early 1954, when GDP registered negative.

From a low point (trough) in 1954, the economy gathered steam to expand, with GDP on nearly a straight-line ride to 1955 to form a picture-perfect peak, and then began the next contraction to the trough in 1958, followed by an expansion to end the decade.

Flash forward five decades for the GDP expansions and contractions from the late 1990s and through the 2000 decade to date. As Figure 1.5 shows, the expansions and contractions are clearly discernible as GDP growth increases and diminishes. The world from this view has not changed from the time when Barbie and Hula Hoops

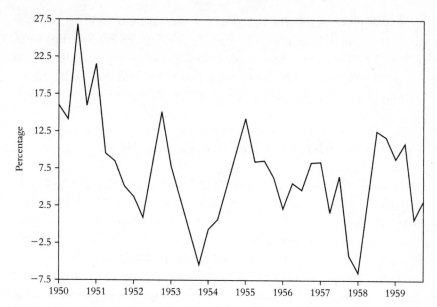

Figure 1.4   GDP Chart Showing Percent Change, Year Over Year, in the 1950s
SOURCE: Bureau of Economic Analysis.

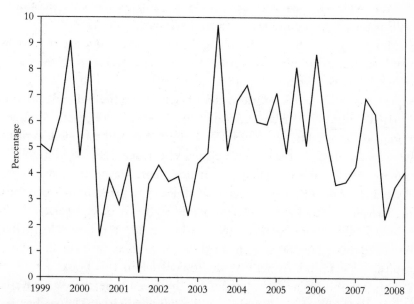

Figure 1.5   GDP Chart, Showing Percent Change, Year Over Year, from 1999 into 2008
SOURCE: Bureau of Economic Analysis.

were new products, to the age of iPods that surf the Internet. What is discernibly different, however, is the length of time between the stages. In the 1950s, we saw two contractions between three peaks. From the late 1990s to the late 2000s were two peaks and two contractions, including one slow meltdown from 2004 to 2008.

Always a Bull Inside the Bear

Given the cyclicality of the economy, we know that even when it looks as if we're entering a bottomless pit and things won't *ever* get better, they will. A contraction will eventually exhaust itself, depleted inventories will call for increased production, employment will rise, and the economy will begin expanding again. And just when we think things are *so* good that it will last this way forever—that the economy can just keep expanding like a balloon made of some space-age elastomer—the expansion will get out of hand. We'll hit the peak and then begin to contract, or else some sector or industry (think dot-com, the credit market) will overexpand and a bubble will inflate. Then the economy will snap back into contraction to get itself back on track.

Like waves on the ocean, rolling in and washing out, it's the cycles that keep things, in the long run, on an even keel. So too with the economy, which even when the market is contracting and the bear is reigning supreme, you know it's only a matter of time when the bull will emerge. But that's not all. In *every* economic phase—expansion, peak, contraction, and trough—there is always an opportunity to be tapped. Perhaps it's a sector that's hot when everything else is ice cold. Maybe gold is moving higher in an inflationary environment. Maybe corn prices are skyrocketing because of weather-related delays in planting that will hurt the harvest. Or stocks are up when bonds are down, or vice versa.

As I said before, there is always a bull inside the bear. No matter what the rhyme, reason, or climate, there is always an investment opportunity to be found. As will be discussed later in this book, whatever sectors and industries are expanding at any given time, there are investment vehicles to take advantage of these opportunities. The exchange-traded fund (ETF) allows investors to take advantage of price moves in a particular index, sector, or industry, from the broad-based Standard

& Poor's 500 (ETF symbol SPY) to something much more narrow like solar-energy (with the clever symbol of TAN). So rather than stockpiling gold bars in your basement because you think precious metal prices are going up, you can buy a gold ETF (GLD). Like agribusiness? Then MOO—that's the symbol. As you'll read later on, I believe the development of the ETF is the most significant investment revolution since the put.

The Role of the Fed

As we study the world for what has changed and what stays the same, we must keep an eye on the Federal Reserve, which over the past four decades has been led by three distinctive chairmen, who differ in personality, temperament, leadership style, and the economic climates they face. The Fed has utilized a variety of tools to heat up or cool down the economy, depending upon what was necessary.

What remains steadfastly the same is the role of the Fed. The Federal Reserve has a stated mandate to promote price stability, full employment, and noninflationary growth. It has, in my opinion, limited tools to address these goals. Of course the Fed can raise or lower rates, and add liquidity into the system through open market operations or, more recently, through the term auction facility (TAF) program, swaps, and so forth.

One of my favorite Fed weapons is to increase or decrease the reserve requirements of member banks. All this can do in reality, however, is instill confidence in the system, because market dynamics are truly The Force behind the cost of money. For example, in early 2008 when the Fed wanted—no, actually needed—to lower rates in a hurry in response to the credit crisis, short-term rates actually went *up* as the Fed lowered the Fed funds rate and the discount rate (see Figure 1.6).

As the role of the Fed morphs with the evolution of the economy, there will be debate over just how much power the Fed should have. For example, did the Fed exert too much control with respect to orchestrating the rescue of Bear Stearns, taking over Freddie Mac and Fannie Mae, providing an initial $85 billion in financing to AIG, and then the $700 billion bailout of Wall Street? Is it the Fed's mandate to oversee financial institutions that are not member banks? Should the Fed

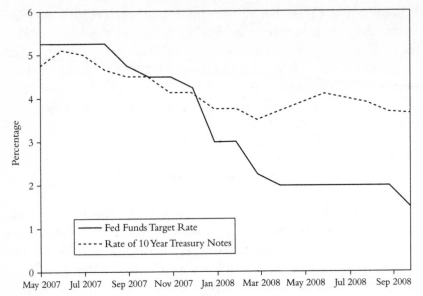

Figure 1.6   Fed Rate Cuts in 2008 Were Ineffective at Lowering Long-Term
Interest Rates
SOURCE: U.S. Board of Governors of the Federal Reserve System; Federal Reserve Board of
Governors.

allow nonmembers to borrow at the discount window? Add to the
list any number of questions of how the landscape of the markets, business, and the role of the Fed has changed forever.

New tools and policies, and new faces in the role of chairman—
all of it will make a mark on the power, control, and influence of the
Federal Reserve. That has changed over time, and will most likely
continue to in the years and decades ahead. What remains the same,
however, is the role of the Fed when it comes to price stability, full
employment, and noninflationary growth. That mission does not
change. How the Fed manages to accomplish that, however, will be
altered over time.

In the past, I believed that too much emphasis was put on watching the Fed as it had limited powers to influence the economy. Raising
or lowering the fed funds rate, changes in the discount window, and
changes in reserve requirements for member banks were the tools in
the Fed workshop. As the economy matured and other instruments
met the needs for the marketplace (commercial paper, capital markets,

etc.), the Fed's influence over rates remained in question, at least to me. After all, it was not as if the Fed could buy my house, grant me a mortgage, or find me a job. Rather, it could in some small way stimulate the economy, which would have the trickle-down effect. I remember an article I wrote entitled "Ignore the Man behind the Curtain," in which I called the Fed a fiscal post office whose function was to make sure liquidity flowed and that my checks cleared.

Well, has that all changed! I guess the Fed *can* buy my house, or at least my bad cash investments. Actually I think they could buy or at least swap my house for cash if I was an investment bank or another firm whose existence was essential to the daily functioning of life as we know it. The Fed has suddenly exercised or, along with the Treasury Department, has been given powers that can impact the economy more directly, at least in the short run. The jury is out on the success of these measures and the true damage to your life and mine if some of these "too big to fail" institutions really did fail. But the bottom line is the Fed now has more powers to influence short-term economic fundamentals. Let's see if it really can change the weather.

The World As We Know It

While the world has not changed, differences can be perceived as one cycle comes to an end and another begins. In early 2008 employment trends indicated an economic cycle change. Long before it showed up in GDP, we noticed the signs in employment first. No one could have predicted the severity of it. But truth be told, jobs were not being created at a pace that would support the economic growth and, therefore, stock prices as we saw then. As Figure 1.7 shows, GDP growth, from quarter to quarter, slowed considerably in Q4 2007 and Q1 2008.

For some, this meant more than just a contraction or slowdown. Warren Buffett proclaimed in March 2008 that the U.S. economy was already in a recession "by a common sense definition," even if it didn't meet the technical definition of two consecutive quarters of negative growth.[2]

While GDP indicated an economic contraction and the Oracle of Omaha was preaching recession, these were not the top concerns for

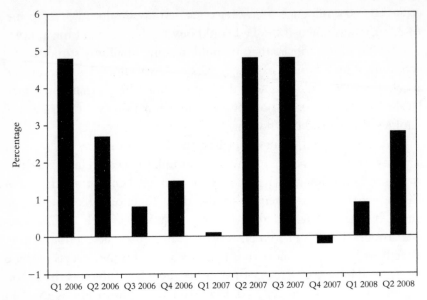

Figure 1.7   Quarter-to-Quarter Growth in Real GDP
SOURCE: Bureau of Economic Analysis.

most people. In fact, if you asked people what their biggest concern was in mid-2008, it was a good bet that they would have said energy prices.

When gasoline prices rose well above $4 a gallon—something that was not only unprecedented, but was once unthinkable—energy costs became front-and-center on consumers' minds. And while, as a consumer, I had my share of sticker-shock when I filled up the tank of my car, as an economist, I knew that energy prices were *not* the biggest factor driving inflation at that time.

Energy was still a smaller percentage of consumer spending than it was years ago. Yes, it was significant, and the media made a point of showcasing lower-middle-class Americans who were making the tough choice between filling up the tank and buying groceries. High pump prices and emotional impact aside, energy prices did not escalate all that much when you compare them to wages.

For example, in 1979, the average gasoline price was $0.943 per gallon, and the average hourly wage was $6.343, for a gas-to-earnings ratio of roughly 0.149. By 1981, gas prices had run up to an average of $1.41 per gallon, while average hourly wages also rose to about $7.438, for a gas-to-wages ratio of 0.190.

Table 1.1   Average Gasoline Prices, Average Wages, and Gas-to-Wage Ratio for 1980, 1990, 2000 to mid–2008

	Gas (US$)	Hourly Earnings (US$)	Gas/Hourly Earnings (%)
1980	1.27	6.85	18.5120
1990	1.28	10.20	12.5321
2000	1.64	14.01	11.7291
2001	1.56	14.54	10.7032
2002	1.56	14.97	10.4129
2003	1.70	15.37	11.0950
2004	1.94	15.69	12.3492
2005	2.49	16.12	15.4313
2006	2.74	16.75	16.3814
2007	2.99	17.42	17.1472
Mid-2008	3.84	17.85	21.1513

SOURCE: Oil Price Information Service (OPIS); U.S Bureau of Labor Statistics.

By early summer 2008 with gasoline rising to levels that made motorists actually think about walking (proving that the numbers at the pump are a more powerful motivator than other numbers such as weight, waist measurement, and cholesterol levels), one might have expected that the gas-to-wage ratio had skyrocketed. Right? Wrong. As Table 1.1 shows, the escalation in average wages has tempered the bite from the rise in gasoline.

Thus, in this book, when discussing energy, we need to make the distinction that while crude oil and gasoline prices were high, they were not the biggest inflationary factor. (And with gas prices sinking to below $2 per gallon on the national average in late 2008, it appears that the inflationary impact of energy is the least of our problems.) When prices go high enough, demand is curtailed, and prices fall. These are the classic supply-and-demand forces at work.

By contrast, wages are the biggest—and most worrisome—cause of inflation. Wages are inelastic on the downside and don't fluctuate as easily as energy prices. It takes a full-on recession and an increase in unemployment to 6.5 percent to even curtail wage growth. By acknowledging that, we leave the door open for supply shock inflation and monetary inflation—the kind that damage the economy because of wage pressure or monetary policy.

Today's World and Money Supply

While the world has not changed fundamentally, there has been a significant change the impact of which will be felt for decades to come. We are now—and I know you are sick of this phrase—a global economy. That means more than the shoes on your feet imported from Italy, the coffee in your cup from beans grown in South America, and so forth. Money supply growth in the United States can cause bubbles elsewhere. Growth in China and India can offset weakness in Europe. Cheap labor in developing countries can offset inflation in the United States. Therefore, we need to be mindful of global imbalances such as wage growth, money supply growth, and currency pegs (read: manipulation) that even a decade ago would barely cause a blip on the U.S. economy.

As we'll explore later in the book, one of the significant attributes of our current times is the aggressive bubble that developed in credit and liquidity. This was created from a global increase in money supply and world output—the latter being the excuse of why we can leverage without worry and why a slowdown in the United States would be offset by growth somewhere else. Therefore investors need not worry, as a new sucker was born every minute to feed the insatiable thirst for liquidity. (See Figure 1.8.)

Conclusion: A Changing, Consistent World

So has the world changed? We have become a global economy and sophisticated tools exist to monitor and shape the world's economies. However, the recurring cycles of expansion, peak, contraction, and trough, have not changed—thankfully. We need all four for a healthy economy, the contraction just as much as the expansion, even though most people think of contraction as "negative" or "bad for the economy." (Not fun, perhaps, but definitely not bad.) Trying to avoid contractions would be like eliminating winter in favor of endless summer. That might sound good on paper, but would cause devastating results for the other three seasons (not to mention the ski resorts).

Even the severe fallout from the credit crisis has carried some good lessons that apparently needed to be learned the hard way: identifying

Figure 1.8 Money Supply (M2) Spiked in the Late 1990s and Early 2000s, but Inflation (as Measured by the Consumer Price Index, or CPI) Did Not Follow. Rather, CPI and Wages Have Been More in Lockstep
SOURCE: U.S. Bureau of Labor Statistics; Federal Reserve.

and managing risk; being prudent in lending and borrowing; and the need for new regulations (for starters I would advocate changes in mark-to-market accounting to avoid massive writedowns of depreciating assets). At the risk of adopting a Pollyanna view, we need the difficult times to get rid of the fat and the excesses, which will eventually allow us to emerge stronger and more efficient.

The recurring cycles of expansion, peak, contraction, and trough are most pronounced when viewing the economy as a whole. Employment trends and output trends measured by GDP and the employment report are most reflective of the overall economy. Historically (or within my reference points of the 1970s through the present), investment choices and allocation decisions vacillated between stocks, bonds, and real estate (housing). In fact, if we look at the price appreciation over the last 25 to 30 years you will most likely see a very similar total return from all of these assets.

However, the paths to the returns were very different. Equities enjoyed what some call the longest bull run on record as the U.S. economy enjoyed an extended period of low inflation and declining rates along with tax code changes and savings incentives that promoted stock investments. Housing lagged equity investments for a decade or so until demand accelerated as criteria for home ownership and first-time buyers became more flexible as the risk of default was mitigated by securitization of loans. Home ownership was not reflective of long-term plans; therefore temporary ownership was suddenly acceptable, which created more demand. During the last 10 years or so housing outpaced equities as the NASDAQ bubble popped and housing became the seemingly more practical investment, thanks to lower mortgage rates and an even greater population of potential buyers who supported higher housing prices.

The overperformance in equities of the 1990s was followed by a decline and then a long period of flat to nonexistent appreciation. Although it was to be expected, it's hard to believe it actually happened as many thought we were in the midst of a new paradigm of the ever-expanding market. Now that the housing market has significantly outperformed for the past decade and the contraction is well under way it's clear that the fate suffered by the equity markets is being shared by the housing markets: a hard drop to eliminate the froth followed by a long period of flat pricing with little or no appreciation. Although there are many good reasons to own a home for the long haul, investment and quick appreciation will not be among them.

As I stated earlier in the chapter, the next opportunity will emerge as stocks finally take the lead as the investment of choice and return for the next expansion. With a higher interest rate environment about to begin and housing still suffering from oversaturation, overleverage, and overvaluation, equities will be investors' first choice.

Additionally, as greater diversity of financial assets through ETFs and other exchange-traded securities mature further, investors will have a greater selection of securities to use—resulting in a more efficient and targeted approach that will have benefits beyond a broad equity investment. Investors can invest in specific areas of the economy that are expanding without having to have exposure to areas that are contracting. This will be a very exciting next 10 years.

Chapter 2

Bubbles, Bursts, and Blips

A View of the Past

Since history is the greatest teacher, we can learn much from events of the past. Specific to this book are significant events that occurred within certain markets or sectors, roughly one per each of the decades we are focusing on, from the 1970s through the 2000s. In some cases, such as gold in the 1970s and tech stocks in the 1990s, a bona fide bubble was created: an expansion (bull market) that overextended itself beyond rational limits. Whenever there is a bubble, it is only a matter of time before it bursts, although when that happens is usually anyone's guess. As the quotation attributed to John Maynard Keynes so aptly observes, "The market can stay irrational longer than you can stay solvent." When the bubble does burst, the impact will either be narrow, within a particular sector, or more widespread, depending upon the dynamics and participation at the time.

In other points in time, what occurred was not a bubble and a burst, but rather a "blip." An event that may have seemed like a bigger deal at the time in retrospect proved not to be a long-term and widespread market disruption after all, nor was there any significant impact on the economy. And then there are the scapegoat events that get blamed for a slowing economy or a recession, but which actually allow businesses to cut fire and reload. An example is September 11th, which while tragic on a human and social scale, did not put the stock market into decline and the economy into recession. The market correction and slowing economy were happening anyway.

In the midst of the events as they unfold, however, it is hard to gain and keep perspective. During expansions, even when there is evidence that a bubble is inflating, a speculative euphoria can result, making people think that the good times will continue to roll forever—just like that dot-com stock somebody bought in 1999 thinking it could just keep doubling in value without ever correcting. And during the bursts, the snapback can be so sharp and so painful that people think the sky is falling, when all that's really happening is prices are descending rapidly toward more rational values.

With the passage of time comes the intellectual and emotional ability to see more clearly; first, to identify what was really a bubble—an expansion that went beyond reasonable limits and expectations until it burst—and what was really a blip, or a temporary upset caused by other outside forces or a momentary disequilibrium.

Examining events of the past, not only can we see just what constitutes a bubble and what does not, but we can learn other lessons as well. The most obvious one is that, as history has clearly shown, bubbles and blips can and do develop. As we look ahead, it's only a matter of time before another one occurs—and later in this book I'll explore just such an example where I see the next bubble forming and why.

We can also see what contributes to bubbles; not only speculative fever, but also the prevailing monetary policy at the time. Additionally, I believe there are societal and behavioral changes that take place simultaneously, encouraging and promoting bubble mania. Being aware of all the contributing factors helps us become both forewarned and prepared in advance of the next bubble.

The 1970s: The Gold Bubble Inflates

By the early 1970s, there was widespread acceptance of the fact that the United States needed to move completely off the gold standard. The country had been on the gold standard since 1879, but many changes had taken place since then. In 1933, in the aftermath of the Great Depression, President Roosevelt put several restrictions on gold, including forbidding banks to pay out gold or to export it. The government also increased its supply of gold, which allowed it to inflate money supply. In April 1933, Roosevelt ordered all gold coins and gold certificates in denominations of $100 or more to be turned in and exchanged for money at a set price of $20.67 per ounce. In 1934, the government's price of gold was increased to $35 per ounce—a price that was held until August 15, 1971. On that date, President Nixon announced that the United States would no longer convert dollars to gold at a fixed rate, which completely abandoned the gold standard. In 1974, President Ford signed a law permitting Americans to own gold bullion.[1]

In the aftermath of these monetary policy changes, gold prices, which previously had been controlled, were suddenly allowed to move. Investors and speculators now had greater access to own gold than ever before. When prices of any commodity that have been artificially kept low are suddenly allowed to move, what often occurs is a dramatic spike in one direction. In the case of the gold, as shown in Figure 2.1, prices went swiftly higher from artificially low levels, as pent-up demand at the fixed price—which was well below equilibrium. Further, the fixed gold price was insulated from supply/demand forces and, therefore, out of sync with the market. At the time, some non-U.S. investors had found a way to buy and sell gold at a far greater price.

The Developing Economy

Economically and socially, there were other developments that impacted the dollar and its speculative counterpart, gold. For one, the U.S. economy was becoming more developed. Changes were occurring that indicated the start of the shift from manufacturing to a service economy. The maturing of the post-World War II workforce created

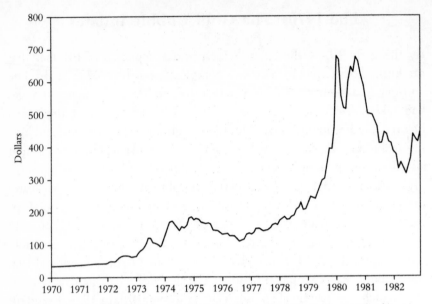

Figure 2.1 Monthly Average Gold Prices Show the Quick, Steep Climb as Speculative Fever Hit the Market after Prices Were No Longer Held at Artificially Low Levels
SOURCE: http://www.kitco.com.

a larger number of white-collar workers who were in higher paying supervisory and management positions. Figure 2.2 shows that wages were on the rise, which added to inflationary pressure, particularly due to cost-of-living adjustments (COLA) that were embedded in employment and labor contracts.

Specific to gold was tremendous pent-up demand, particularly from investors. As prices were allowed to float, the forces of supply and demand could exert their influence. The market moved, and when it did, it brought in speculators. Put it all together—increased money supply, inflation, and speculators rushing to buy, sell, trade, and cash in gold—and you have all the classic makings of a bubble.

As prices rose through the 1970s, people scoured their households for gold to sell. Grandpa's watch and Grandma's ring were unearthed from drawers and keepsake boxes. It didn't matter if it was 14-, 18- or 24-carat, as long as it glittered it could be cashed in.

The bull market that developed in gold fueled speculation, partially because it was being used as a hedge during a time of double-digit

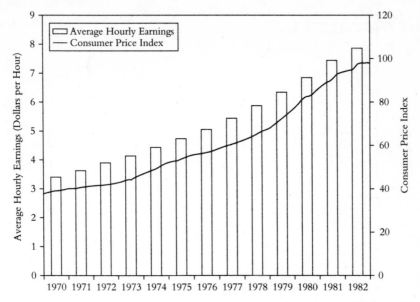

Figure 2.2   Hourly Earnings on the Rise in the 1970s Adding to Inflationary Pressures
SOURCE: Federal Reserve Bank of St. Louis: FRED; Bureau of Labor Statistics.

inflation. Gold also became an investment favorite as the dollar traded sharply lower. In October 1979, gold soared an unbelievable (at the time) $50 an ounce in two days to trade at over $447, closing for the week at $385. As *Time* magazine quoted a New York bullion trade at the time, "The market's gone bananas."[2]

The Incredibly Shrinking Dollar

The real concern was not the price of gold, but the shrinking value of the dollar. This was the era of whipping double-digit inflation and trying to stabilize the dollar, including with so-called "Carter Bonds," which were a series of U.S. Treasuries issued by the United States in 1978 to prevent the fall of the dollar.

At an International Monetary Fund meeting in the fall of 1979, Treasury Secretary G. William Miller and Federal Reserve Chairman Paul Volcker were confronted with pleas from other nations to intervene. One of the actions considered was to increase gold sales by the government: specifically, that the United States might double the 750,000

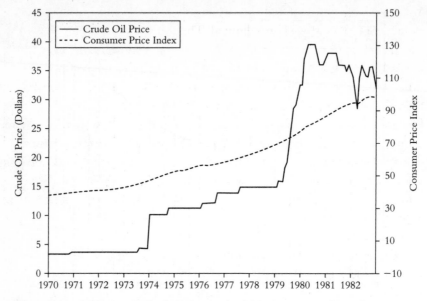

Figure 2.3   Oil Prices Spiked Higher in the 1970s Because of Supply
Disruptions—Not a Speculative Bubble
Source: Federal Reserve Bank of St. Louis: FRED; Bureau of Labor Statistics.

ounces of Fort Knox bullion that the country then sold per month.
Under Secretary of the Treasury Anthony Solomon indicated the
action was possible, saying the gold boom was extremely unhealthy for
the world economy.

This is the classic bubble talk—far different from, say, the oil price
shock caused by the 1973 Arab Oil Embargo when members of the
Organization of Arab Petroleum Exporting Countries (OAPEC—not
to be confused with the broader OPEC) announced they would no
longer ship oil to countries that had supported Israel in its conflict with
Egypt and Syria, known as the Yom Kippur War or the Arab-Israeli War.
As oil prices spiked, there were calls for cuts in consumption. The reason? Prices were not skyrocketing (as shown in Figure 2.3) because of
a speculative bubble, but rather the reaction to a supply disruption.

As for the speculative gold bubble, after the price spike in the early
1980s, there was a quick sell off, followed by a prolonged period of flat
prices. After topping out at $850 an ounce on January 21, 1980, gold spent
about 20 years trading essentially around $350 an ounce. What's interest-
ing to note is what happened when the gold market contracted sharply.

Yes, there were undoubtedly some speculators who got burned, but for most people the impact was limited. They simply put grandpa's pocket watch back in the drawer or decided not to sell grandma's ring after all.

While the gold market of the 1970s had the characteristics of any other bubble, including fevered speculation, its disruption wasn't pervasive from an economic standpoint. From a sociological perspective, the gold price rise provided what my grandfather used to call "mad money"—extra funds to spend. So when prices declined all that was damaged was people's extra spending money, not their overall net worth or the value of their homes. As we'll see in upcoming time frames, when speculation involves retirement savings or one's largest asset, such as a home—and a greater population of people are caught up in the net—there is much more potential for widespread damage.

To recap the 1970s, the forces at work included inflation from excessive monetary growth from earlier in the decade (including financing the Vietnam War) and a move off the gold standard that created pent-up demand, which came together to create an expansion and then a bubble in the gold market. Inflation was forced under control with higher rates and a tightening of money supply growth, which ushered in a long period of low or declining rates, low inflation, and continued economic growth.

NOW Accounts and Money Markets

While gold prices were gyrating in the 1970s and into the early 1980s, there was another development: the Negotiable Order of Withdrawal (NOW) account—which pays interest while allowing checks to be written against the balance. The NOW accounts began in Massachusetts in the early 1970s when a group of banks found a loophole in regulations that had prohibited paying interest on checking accounts. The NOW concept soon spread to other banks as the appeal of offering this product to customers caught on.

Another banking product that captured attention was money market accounts. The high interest rate environment at the time made money markets very attractive and appropriate for investors. Money market accounts were paying upwards of 10 percent, which for investors was a great return.

With interest paid on accounts becoming more competitive—and consumers becoming increasingly rate conscious—banks had to become more aggressive with their balance sheets and loan portfolios in order to continue to make the spread that, previously, could be accomplished by simply offering a free toaster to new depositors. As a result, banks and savings and loan (S&L) institutions would lobby the Office of the Comptroller of the Currency and the Federal Reserve for more flexibility, which would eventually lead to them taking more risk. The result was the S&L crisis of the 1980s and 1990s. But first, there were other developments on our economic timeline: a double-dip recession and a "crash" that was really a blip.

The 1980s: Two Dips and a Blip

The era of the 1980s was ushered in with some painful medicine that had to be administered by the Federal Reserve, under the chairmanship of Paul Volcker, to whip inflation that topped 11 percent on an annualized basis by the fourth quarter of 1980. While the Fed's policies and actions essentially caused the often-cited double-dip recession—occurring between 1980 and 1982—there were positive benefits and outcomes in terms of setting the economy up for a long run of expansion, which even the so-called Crash of 1987 could not derail, in spite of dire predictions at the time of another 1929-style recession.

During the economic expansion of the 1980s, the gilded age of Wall Street was beginning. The whole of Wall Street was being recognized as the engine of the economy. The importance of the financial sector had been overlooked somewhat in previous decades. In the 1970s, Wall Street certainly didn't have the same allure as Corporate America and the stalwart names like Sears, Roebuck and General Electric. Company owners, while not on par with the manufacturing and railroad barons of the past, had more prestige than someone who was seen as shuffling papers or moving assets.

It wasn't until the 1980s that investment banking was perceived as a desirable occupation, attracting job seekers out of places like Harvard Business School. Many of the bond kings and trading gods of the 1980s got their start in the 1970s when these jobs were viewed as being more mundane and even less desirable. All that would change in the 1980s, with mergers, acquisitions, and the mythical Gordon Gekko—Hollywood's glamorized version of a corporate raider—telling us that "greed is good." Computer technology started to make trading sexier and attracted brainpower to make it more sophisticated. This was the time of junk bond financing and clever deal structures.

I was in Chicago for most of the early 1980s, working as an analyst for the Federal Reserve. While at the Chicago Fed, I felt far removed from the action in New York, which was clearly where I, as a twenty-something, wanted to be. When my boss sent me to New York to work part of the time, I was definitely a step closer, but still removed. While at the New York Fed, I was fortunate to spend some time on the repo desk, where I interacted with the big investment banks, even if it was just to call to get an update on a currency price, or perhaps to do a transaction for the balance sheet. Still, I felt like I was looking out of a window; I wasn't part of the scene.

As I traveled back and forth from Chicago to New York, I knew I had to make a move, even if it meant being without a job for a time. (Had I been fully cognizant of the impact of the 1982 recession just a few years before, perhaps I wouldn't have been so cavalier with my employment, but such is the insulation of the college years and the folly of youth.)

As this young man prepared to go east, I asked my boss if I could have a list of banks we dealt with regularly, along with the names and addresses of the chief dealers at the banks. I moved to New York without a job and started my letter-writing campaign to every single name on that list. I certainly wasn't alone in my quest for a coveted job on the Street. Everybody, it seemed, wanted to work at Bear Stearns, Kidder Peabody, Goldman Sachs, and the other big houses. My letters resulted in calls from a handful and an offer from one, Bank of America, to join its trading program. So there I was in 1984: a currency trader, living and working in New York.

Wall Street was *the* place to be, with the stock market basking in the glow of an economy that was healthy again. The GDP, which registered −1.9 percent in 1982 (on an annualized basis from the prior period), grew by +4.5 percent in 1983 and +7.4 in 1984, followed by growth that topped 3 percent and 4 percent in each of the remaining years of the decade of the 1980s, as Figure 2.4 illustrates.

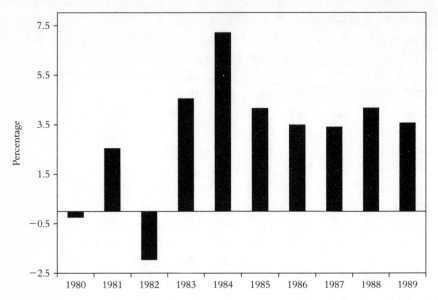

Figure 2.4   Annualized GDP Performance (on a Percentage Basis Compared to Prior Period) for the Decade of the 1980s
SOURCE: Bureau of Economic Analysis.

401(k) Plans Expand Market Participation

While the stock market was not as widely followed as it is today—as most folks watch the Dow the way people used to keep track of baseball scores—market participation had broadened somewhat in the 1980s. People started becoming more market-savvy thanks to the 1978 change in the Internal Revenue Code that stated employees would not be taxed on deferred compensation (as opposed to direct compensation). That led to the proliferation of a retirement plan known as the 401(k), which allows employees to contribute pretax dollars to retirement accounts, with a percentage often matched by employers. As employees signed up for 401(k) plans and selected from a menu of mutual funds, for many of them it was their introduction to the equities market.

The launch of the 401(k) plan forever changed investor behavior and has had a profound impact on the economy. For one, deferred compensation plans took a little of the pressure off the government when it came to Social Security. Further, participants began to feel as if they had some control over their retirements. However, the fact that they were contributing to a 401(k) plan probably meant they were saving less out of their paychecks. While I don't want to diminish the importance of people accumulating retirement savings out of pretax dollars, some folks decided they could just "spend the rest." Why save any more, if they were already contributing to a 401(k)? This led to a very careless attitude among consumers in general about money, spending, and saving (or lack thereof).

Fundamentally, the proliferation of 401(k) plans and other retirement vehicles also increased the demand for stocks. As people opted into plans and made their selections for mutual funds, money began flowing into the coffers of fund managers who had to buy stock to stay fully invested. Now a new metric that I call "demand for stock" was created, which would add another dimension when analyzing a stock price beyond price-to-earnings (P/E) levels, strong earnings, or favorable fundamentals. Simply because funds flowed into accounts on a regular basis, fund managers had to buy stock.

With greater and broader participation in the market thanks to the 401(k), the Federal Reserve and the Treasury had even more reason to make sure the stock market stayed positively sloped over time. The stock market and retail investment became another indirect tool to help smooth out economic speed bumps. This would later become part of the fuel that inflated another bubble in a decade or so—and would become an incentive behind some monetary policy moves. But first came the blip.

The Un-Crash of 1987

On so-called Black Monday, October 19, 1987, the doomsayers began to preach that "no one remembered the Depression," which, as they saw it, was where we were headed. By this time I was in Chicago, trading currencies. Although I saw absolute panic in the market that day, in hindsight the market did not "crash." Even though the Dow Jones Industrial Average dropped 508 points to 1739—a loss of more than 22 percent in one day—the stock market had *not* been in a bubble, nor was this a burst. In fact, I wouldn't call it a crash at all.

In order to gain more perspective on Black Monday, let's take a look at what happened just prior. On Friday October 16, the stock

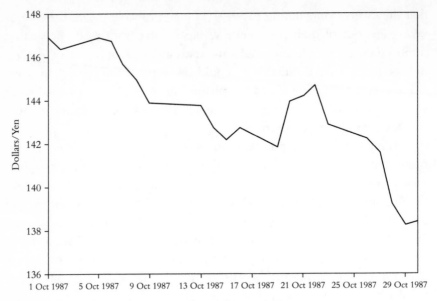

Figure 2.5   The Japanese Yen vs. the Dollar in 1987
SOURCE: Board of Governors of the Federal Reserve System.

market took a beating. The Dow closed at 2246.73, down 108.36 points from the prior day—or a loss of 4.6 percent. At the time, the United States was engaged in tense talks with the Germans over the U.S. dollar and trade policies. The U.S. Treasury Secretary, James Baker, criticized Germany for failing to stimulate its economy. The dollar took off, and the stock market got slammed. On Monday, October 19, 1987, the dollar rallied steeply and the trade balance—which was closely watched by currency traders and in other markets—was even further out-of-hand (see Figures 2.5 and 2.6).

Black Monday

On Black Monday I witnessed a veritable flight to quality as bonds went limit-up. Computer programs and portfolio insurance were not as sophisticated as they have become since then. As the market went down things went haywire. The result was the equivalent of everyone panicking and hitting the sell button at once. This was not a crash, but program trading gone awry. System failure might be a better description. The economy wasn't in trouble. The GDP was positive, and the economy

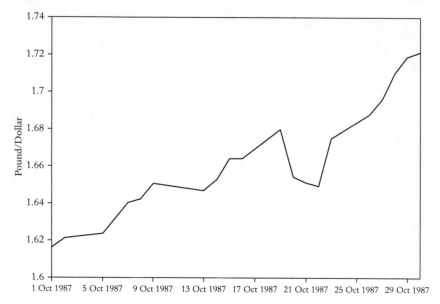

Figure 2.6   The British Pound vs. the Dollar in 1987
SOURCE: Board of Governors of the Federal Reserve System.

was expanding. In fact, it would keep expanding longer than we would think possible.

Nonetheless, the October 1987 stock market decline would become one of those "where were you when it happened" moments. I can remember clearly going into the office early on Black Monday given what had happened in the markets on the previous Friday. Needless to say, I stayed at the office very late on Monday, stunned as everyone else by the fact that the stock market had just dropped some 500 points. I feared what might happen next.

As I left my office in the Chicago Board of Trade building, I walked to the White Hen Pantry convenience store to buy a soda and then stopped at Walgreen's to get toothpaste. I remember looking at the clerks behind the counters and thinking, "Your lives have changed forever and you don't know it yet." They smiled, handed me my change, and told me to have a nice evening.

The disparity between my fears of what could come next and their nonchalance stayed with me. Looking back, it was symbolic of what I would come to realize: the "crash" of 1987 was only a hiccup exacerbated

Figure 2.7   In Retrospect the "Crash" of 1987 Was a Short-Term Correction, with the Market Steadily Recovering Lost Ground
SOURCE: Dow Jones & Company: www.djindexes.com; 200-Day Moving Average; Reproduced with permission of Yahoo! Inc. ® 2008 by Yahoo! Inc. YAHOO! and the YAHOO! logo are trademarks of Yahoo! Inc.

by program trading systems going haywire and dumping holdings en masse. The economy hadn't derailed and we weren't headed into the next Great Depression. Another crisis in a few years would have the potential to push us to that brink. As for this steep, one-day correction—as costly as it was—it was really only a blip, and within a few days the market was back on its way to regaining lost ground (see Figure 2.7).

The Fed to the Rescue

In reaction to the so-called Crash of 1987, Federal Reserve Chairman Alan Greenspan stepped in and immediately lowered rates. This included reversing a rate hike made the week before in response to the situation with the dollar and the trade imbalance, which had put the market into a bit of a tailspin. Overall, the Fed's stance was to set rates that were accommodative, not restrictive.

The economy didn't skip a beat during or after the "blip of '87." While there were losses on account statements, the prevailing buy-and-hold philosophy told people to stay the course and that time would make it up. Housing had not yet become a barometer of economic well-being; it was merely a fact—you either owned your own home or you didn't. Although real estate in the second half of the 1980s would go into recession in places like California and New York, it was not a widespread decline.

S&Ls and Easy Money

The bigger story of the 1980s was the savings and loan (S&L) crisis. Through much of the 1970s, market interest rate fluctuations caused difficulties for S&L institutions, which had to deal with interest rate ceilings that prevented them from paying competitive rates on deposits. When market interest rates rose, S&Ls saw substantial funds withdrawn by consumers to be placed elsewhere to earn a higher rate of return. Money market funds and "NOW" accounts posed considerable competition.

Although we couldn't see it then, the NOW account resulted in very important changes in depositors' actions and behavior. The quest for more and more return and the pressure on banks to make more to pay out more would be the beginning of banking problems that would surface decades later.

The 1980s also saw new regulatory changes being enacted, including the ability to invest in land development and other speculative real estate—all of which were aimed at helping S&Ls improve their profitability. Other changes followed: the Depository Institutions Deregulation and Monetary Control Act removed the interest rates ceiling on deposit accounts and eliminated distinctions among different types of depository institutions. In December 1982, the Garn-St. Germain Depository Institutions Act of 1982 expanded powers of federally chartered S&Ls to diversify their activities to increase profits. This included elimination of deposit interest rate ceilings; elimination of previous statutory limits on loan-to-value ratios; and expansion of asset powers for federal S&Ls, to allow up to 40 percent of assets in commercial mortgages, up to 30 percent in consumer loans, and up to 10 percent in commercial leases.

By the mid- to late-1980s, losses threatened to tumble S&Ls across the country. As the crisis worsened, the Federal Savings and Loan Insurance Corporation (FSLIC), which administered deposit insurance for S&Ls,

became insolvent. Billions in additional taxpayer funds were contributed, but the FSLIC was abolished in 1989 and S&L deposit insurance was transferred to the Federal Deposit Insurance Corporation (FDIC).

By 1989, the S&L crisis was being cleaned up with the Financial Institutions Reform Recovery and Enforcement Act, which switched oversight of S&Ls to a newly created Office of Thrift Supervision. The Resolution Trust Corporation was created to take care of insolvent S&Ls.[3]

The S&L crisis had the potential to cause major defaults and a 1930s style Depression. In fact, if the powers that be had not been able to contain the damage from the S&L crisis, we could have seen a full-blown, widespread economic catastrophe. What many had feared would result from the "crash" of 1987 could very easily have occurred from the S&L crisis. The fact that this didn't happen has always made me feel good about the strong hand of the Fed during the early 1980s to counter inflation, even if it did create a double-dip recession. Paramount was and is the stability of the banking system, which allowed the Fed to utilize its various tools to help the country work its way out of recession. It's like having an IV in place in a seriously ill patient so medicine can be administered immediately.

The federal government's actions during the S&L crisis bailed out the weak banks and pumped money into the system. Further, interest rates were held artificially higher than market forces would have dictated at the time. Plus there were heavy restrictions on banks, essentially setting the spread at which institutions could borrow and loan to the government by buying Treasuries. When banks' balance sheets were declared healthy enough, they were able to make loans again not only to triple-A rated borrowers but also to other creditworthy borrowers as well.

As a result of these actions, there was a price to be paid by the American consumer for the bailout of the banking system. It was not a sticker shock. Rather, there were increases in the cost of just about everything to make up for higher financing costs, but no one seemed to notice they were being "nickeled and dimed." Their mortgage rates were a fact, not a something to be shopped around. There were no adjustable rate mortgages, no jumping from bank to bank to gain a few points. Financing costs overall were higher and consumers paid the difference—unknowingly, I might add. However, consumers would

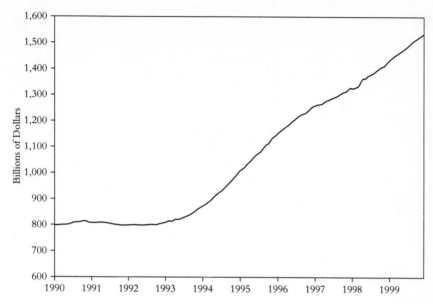

Figure 2.8   As Consumer Credit Goes Up...
SOURCE: U.S. Board of Governors of the Federal Reserve System.

soon be able to play catch-up as banks eventually cleaned up their balance sheets and opened the liquidity window to lower-rated borrowers. This would spur the next economic growth phase as credit expanded by the greatest rate ever, and we let the buying begin. What came next was huge growth in consumer credit, which spurred spending, as shown in Figure 2.8. And as credit grew, savings, as one might imagine, dropped dramatically (Figure 2.9).

The 1980s in Perspective

The 1980s saw a more typical investment climate and garden variety investment choices such as equities and bonds, plus real estate in the form of housing for the long run as a diversifier. The norm was a 30-year mortgage with holding periods over 10 years. The big change in the 1980s was retirement accounts and equity investing: the 401(k) plan, the individual retirement account (IRA), stock options, matching plans, and so forth were all tied to or hinged on the equity markets. This created demand for stock beyond traditional fundamentals. Supply

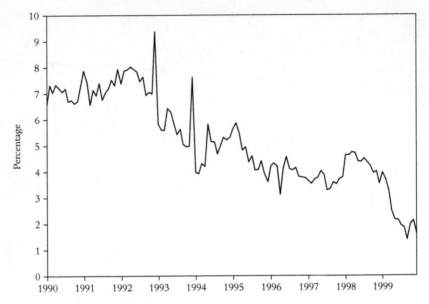

Figure 2.9   Personal Savings Declines
SOURCE: Bureau of Economic Analysis.

was declining as mergers and acquisitions (M&A) activity financed by junk bonds competed with retail investors and won. All this helped keep a steady upward bias to equities for much of the decade.

As retirement accounts and 401(k) plans became the new largest household asset or maybe a close second to one's home, stock market movements had more relevance in deciding monetary policy. And, the impact of rate movements on the stock market was being watched by the average investor—accentuated by CNBC and the rest of the financial media that called stock movements like a horse race. Celebrity status was achieved by market mavens and economists with the latest projections.

Greenspan, the first celebrity Fed chairman, became a household name and his words could move markets. The stock market became a barometer of the economy, and Fed policy moved the stock market. As the "Greenspan effect" became evident, investors felt even more confident in buying stocks that a few decades ago were considered a speculative investment and that should be offset with a generous por-tion of bonds in one's portfolio. This change of saving for retirement by investing in the stock market in a tax-advantaged method cannot be overemphasized for its impact on how we invest and how we view the economic good times. It also became the fuel for the next bubble in the 1990s, as retirement assets became concentrated in tech stocks, as investors considered any stock to be an equity investment and felt a portfolio of dot-coms was just as safe as a portfolio of blue chips.

As more and more retirement portfolios became increasingly weighted to equities, banks and saving accounts suffered. Cheap depositor money was less abundant so banks exercised the more lucrative but riskier investments that eventually caused some banks to become insolvent. The engineered bailout was brilliant. Buyers discovered assets at reasonable discounts; mergers were sought for troubled institutions, and the yield curve was kept steep so banks could borrow cheaply and loan to Triple-A-rated borrowers or U.S. Treasuries. In time, housing loans appeared compelling as banks' balance sheets would allow for more mortgage-related loans, and newfangled risk tools were developed to reduce the risk of default. With the lending window virtually closed to most businesses and consumers for many years, the new liquidity at attractive rates helped ignite the next bull market.

The 1990s: An Expansion Here, a Bubble There

As we entered the 1990s, the banking crisis was on its way to being resolved and the economy was getting on firm footing. A shallow recession in the early 1990s—as GDP dropped into negative territory at −0.2 percent for all of 1991 from +1.9 in 1990—soon ended, and a period of economic expansion followed. The annualized GDP numbers say it all for this decade, as the table below showing GDP percent changes from the previous period illustrates.[4]

1990 + 1.9	1996 + 3.7
1991 − 0.2	1997 + 4.5
1992 + 3.3	1998 + 4.2
1993 + 2.7	1999 + 4.5
1994 + 4.0	2000 + 3.7
1995 + 2.5	

The strength of the economy was bolstered by workforce changes. Not only were there more women in the workforce, but the workforce was generally better educated. As computers became more widespread through the 1980s and 1990s, with a PC on every desk, productivity gains that reached historic levels in the 1980s were not only sustainable, but would continue to advance. So despite the slight recession in the 1990s and the banking crisis, the economy was well and growing through much of that decade.

What happened next set the stage for the long expansion of the 1990s, and also sowed the seeds of both booms and busts to follow. Interest rates were lowered in the 1990s to stimulate the economy, which improved the monetary flow between banks and also resulted in lower *consumer* rates as well. When the Fed lowered its rates, suddenly there was a drop in the interest for credit cards and mortgage rates on a more widespread basis. In the past, when the Fed lowered rates it was a nice benefit to banks that would somehow get passed along to some top "A-1" customers. Now, a lower interest rate environment was benefiting consumers more broadly, with liquidity available to the masses. And we spent and consumed our way into the mid-1990s.

The Tech Bubble

The free flowing liquidity also found its way into the stock market, which was clearly in expansion mode. As shown in Figure 2.10, the broad market was enjoying a strong bull run through the 1990s.

Within certain sectors, particularly in the late 1990s, there was more than just an expansion going on. Tech stocks—especially the dot-coms—experienced extreme growth that was a classic bubble. Investors bought new tech stock issues, some fresh out of initial public offerings (IPOs), which posted huge gains in a short period of time. Blue chips also rallied, but were castigated for not being up 20 percent like their NASDAQ brethren. Amidst all the hopeful talk about a new economy, no one wanted to rain on that parade—except, perhaps, Federal Reserve Chairman Alan Greenspan in his infamously cautionary irrational exuberance speech of 1996 (see also Figure 2.11):

> ...But how do we know when irrational exuberance has unduly escalated asset values, which then become subject to unexpected and prolonged contractions as they have in Japan

Figure 2.10 NASDAQ/S&P Spread Shows Spike in Late 1999–Early 2000s
SOURCE: The Nasdaq Stock Market, Inc. (NASDAQ): NASDAQ.com; Standard & Poor's (S&P): Central Inquiry Office; Moody's Economy.com.

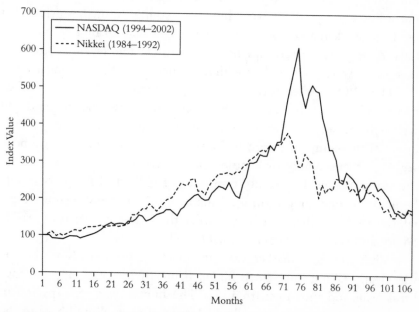

Figure 2.11 Bubbles in the NASDAQ and the Nikkei Show "Irrational Exuberance"
SOURCE: The Nasdaq Stock Market, Inc. (NASDAQ): NASDAQ.com; Nikkei Average Index; Reproduced with permission of Yahoo! Inc. ® 2008 by Yahoo! Inc. YAHOO! and the YAHOO! logo are trademarks of Yahoo! Inc.

over the past decade? And how do we factor that assessment into monetary policy? We as central bankers need not be concerned if a collapsing financial asset bubble does not threaten to impair the real economy, its production, jobs, and price stability. Indeed, the sharp stock market break of 1987 had few negative consequences for the economy. But we should not underestimate or become complacent about the complexity of the interactions of asset markets and the economy. Thus, evaluating shifts in balance sheets generally, and in asset prices particularly, must be an integral part of the development of monetary policy.[5]

Although it may have seemed that Greenspan was being a party-pooper, the tech stock bubble, particularly when viewed in retrospect, was clearly a misallocation of resources. At the time, stocks of established companies that were experiencing double-digit growth were not being purchased by investment managers or by individuals for their portfolios because there were hot, new young "growth stories" that used the stock market as a way to get access to easy money. No matter if there were no earnings, let alone a sustainable revenues stream—companies were going public with not much more than a concept.

The IPO market was so active (see Figure 2.12)—and investment dollars were so eager to find new prospects—that in hindsight we might be surprised at some of the issues that were brought public. Some of the companies with IPOs were startups that should have been seeking private equity or venture capital instead of public money via the stock market. The equity portfolios of individual investors should be used for solid, long-term investment—not a source of venture capital. But in an overheated equity market, the lines between IPO, private equity, and venture capital became blurred.

While the broad market was rising in a bona fide expansion, the tide was clearly taking some boats higher than others—over the protective break-wall and into uncharted seas. The bubble was very specific to tech stocks, the most irrationally exuberant of them all. To illustrate, the NASDAQ Composite, which was trading around 750 in January 1995, hit a high of about 5000 in March 2000 (see Figure 2.13). By contrast, the NASDAQ Composite in late 2008 was around 1400.

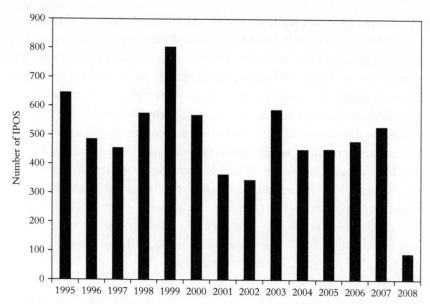

Figure 2.12 IPO Activity Spikes in 1999 and Quickly Falls Off, Mirroring the Tech Bubble Burst
SOURCE: http://bear.cba.ufl.edu/ritter/ipoisr.htm.

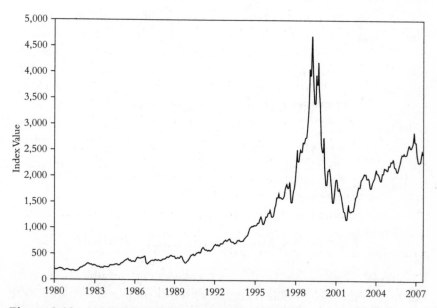

Figure 2.13 NASDAQ Peaks in Early 2000, Followed by a Sharp Decline
SOURCE: The Nasdaq Stock Market, Inc. (NASDAQ): NASDAQ.com.

The relationship between liquidity and the stock market rise is complicated. However, as the tech stocks soared, more of the newfound liquidity found its way into these shares. Financial institutions that had extra money in their coffers increased allocations to trading desks, and where else did the money go except to the hottest game in town?

Don't get me wrong: technology legitimately helped to fuel the economic expansion. Tech-savvy workers became even more productive as they used new tools in new ways, from Excel spreadsheets and Word documents to e-mail. When it came to investing, however, tech was a classic bubble, and it lasted longer than most people would have imagined. If you were smart enough or fortunate enough to have taken your money off the table in 1999 because you saw some warning signs, then the tech market for you was one long ride. If you stayed too long at the amusement park, it wasn't fun anymore.

When the bubble in tech stocks burst, this was not an event with a limited scope as we saw in gold in the 1970s, nor was this a "blip" like the so-called 1987 crash. The tech bubble implosion sent shockwaves through the economy as a whole. First came the final rally sparked by the incredible amount of liquidity dumped into the system to prevent potential Y2K problems, as rumors circulated about glitches in software and computer programs that were expected to cause a crash-and-panic scenario.

Once the market topped, the Fed had to rein in the extra liquidity, which set the stage for a contraction that would inevitably send blue chip stocks into a bear market, with the deflating tech-stock bubble leading the way. While no one could predict when the bubble would burst, it was much easier to spot a bear market or a contraction in the economy, as employment trends would tell the story (see Figure 2.14). By mid-2000, payroll numbers began to decline and shortly thereafter so did the stock market.

The 2000s and the Liquidity Bubble

The new millennium rang in its own set of economic troubles beyond the bursting of the tech bubble. There were the corporate scandals of 2001, involving names like Enron and Worldcom. The terrorist attacks of September 11, 2001, did not bring down the stock market; rather, these

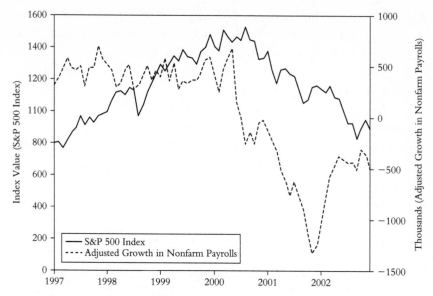

Figure 2.14 As Employment Peaks and Falls, So Does the Stock Market

SOURCE: U.S. Bureau of Labor Statistics, Adjusted statistics computed by Astor Asset Management; Standard & Poor's (S&P): Central Inquiry Office, Moody's Economy.com.

tragic events added downward pressure to what was already a contraction in equities.

The Federal Reserve responded with a plan to rescue the economy by cutting rates lower and lower. By June 2003, the Federal Open Market Committee announced the last in a continuous round of cuts with a 25 basis point reduction in the federal funds rate to 1 percent (see Figure 2.15). As the Fed turned on the liquidity spigot, the money that saturated the economy flowed into a new place. In the previous decade, extra liquidity helped to boost the stock market and further inflate the tech bubble. Investors who had been burned in stocks craved a new bubble in which to invest the extra liquidity.

The Housing Bubble

In the 2000s, money made its way into housing through any of a number of doors. For one, as the Fed cut rates, banks lowered interest rates to make mortgages cheaper and cheaper. With banks able to offer a wider variety of mortgage products, they also became more aggressive

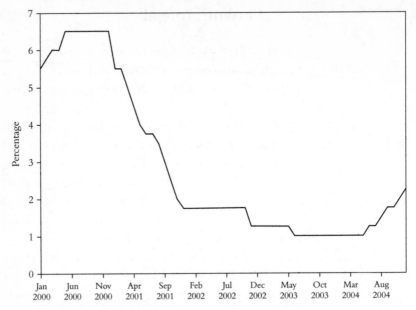

Figure 2.15   Rate Cuts Take the Fed Funds Target Rate Down to 1 Percent—
An Historically Low Level That Holds for Months
SOURCE: Federal Reserve Board of Governors.

to bring in new borrowers, which resulted in an easing of lending
practices. Suddenly, a house was something that *everybody* had to have,
no matter if they lacked the income or the assets to really afford it. No
down payment? No problem! Banks allowed 100 percent financing.
Already have a home? No time like the present to refinance, and while
you're at it, put some of that equity in your home to work by borrowing more and spending the extra cash on furniture, cars, SUVs, and the
other creature comfort "toys" of the conspicuous consumption society.

Housing was hot and prices escalated. Suddenly a house wasn't
just a residence, it was an investment. Ordinary people were buying
houses to "flip." It almost became a sport. Sound irrationally exuberant?
Indeed, as we'll explore in Part II, the liquidity bubble of the 2000s
led to a crisis in the credit and housing markets, with a devastating
bubble-and-burst that impacts an even greater number of people and
that will likely have a bigger and longer-lasting effect on the economy
for longer periods of time than events of the recent past.

Looking Ahead

As history tells us, there will be bubbles in the future—and probably a few blips along the way as well. As we've seen in tech stocks and the housing market, growth in money supply did help create a bubble environment.

With all the liquidity being added to the system to combat the credit crisis, it's inevitable that sometime in the future inflation fears will be reignited. The Federal Reserve typically adopts a more restrictive stance in the face of inflation or inflationary threats. This is the opposite of what happened in the 1990s and earlier in the decade of the 2000s when the Fed could take an accommodative view when it came to interest rates without fear of sparking inflation.

The study of recent decades yields other lessons. As we compare the bubbles of gold in the 1970s, tech stocks in the 1990s, and in housing earlier this decade (which will be explored in more depth in coming chapters), we see the differences in the impact of these events. Gold was narrowly focused and did not cause economic disruption. The bubbles in technology stocks and housing were more widespread as they involved more people and, particularly in the case of housing, went beyond speculative capital.

As George Santayana said, "Those who fail to learn the lessons of history are doomed to repeat them." As bubbles get bigger and a larger number of participants are involved, there will be more devastating consequences on both personal finances and economic conditions overall.

As we have seen, regulatory changes and investor behavior combined with an increase in liquidity or greater demand help ignite bull markets in stocks and then in housing. The sequence of events shows it as one long progression encompassing two bubbles and two bursts. By the late 1990s, investor portfolios had become overweighted in riskier stocks with shaky fundamentals and, as the last push of liquidity hit the system in 2000, the tech stock bubble popped as the economy contracted.

As the Fed reinvigorated the economy and cut rates, investors who had been burned by stocks turned to the housing market for their fix. This helped accelerate the expansion (a bull market) in housing. As credit was given indiscriminately, the bubble inflated and popped in this market, too—as will be discussed in detail in Chapters 4 and 5.

The theme of "one bubble popping creates another bubble" will continue as long as we embrace liquidity as the cure-all. This stance by the Fed was made possible in recent years as inflation remained low (for reasons we will discuss later) and rates could be lowered to almost zero, which would encourage speculation. In this environment bubbles appeared more frequently and each new bubble included a larger and wider range of participants. That is currently the biggest concern, as the number of investors impacted by the latest bubble to pop in housing grows.

The Bull Inside the Bear: The Next Bubble to Burst—and Bull to Emerge

Of the three most popular investments—stocks, bonds, and housing—two have seen bubbles. That leaves the third—bonds—as the next likely place for a bubble to develop and then burst.

The credit markets have been closed to most during 2008 for very different reasons than we saw in the early 1990s when lending policies were tight. In the early 1990s it was a risk issue, like your parents not letting you take the car after dark. The reason for the tight credit markets today is the mechanism has been broken. Short-term funding and overnight lending is nonexistent, even though these functions are needed for the banks to operate. The analogy here is your parents are willing to let you take the car, but it won't start. Either way you can't make it to the bonfire party at Lakewood Place Beach.

Eventually the engine will start again—in banking that is—and liquidity will resume its flow. Artificially high bond prices (thanks to low rates) will eventually begin to come back in line with true inflation expectations. Since investors won't tolerate negative interest rates as the inflation rate is above the interest earned, money will flow out and bonds will collapse. Maybe not collapse, but bond prices will certainly experience a contraction. In late 2008, when the next leg down in the equities market occurred, the bond market bubble expanded further as the flight to quality continued. This will likely add even greater fuel to the contraction to come.

When bonds go into bear territory, it will be time to look for the next bull market (and not a bubble). This time it will be equity market-related, not in real estate, bonds, or credit. As we'll explore in further detail in Part III, the bull inside the bear for the near-term will be in stocks as investors disillusioned by housing and without satisfying returns in bonds will venture back into equities again.

Chapter 3

Inflation

The Factor That Is Always with Us

W hen looking at the economy and making decisions as to how to manage your money, inflation is always an issue. To most people, inflation is a negative factor that makes goods—especially things they need, such as food and gasoline—more expensive. Inflation is what makes it tougher to stretch their dollars.

The fact is inflation is a factor that is nearly always with us, although we may only pay attention during the times it heats up. When we think of inflation we generally visualize the devastating economic period of the late 1970s and early 1980s when "whipping inflation now"—or WIN—became an economic and political mantra. Yet once again reflecting the cyclical nature of the economy, what was a severe problem resulted in some amazing benefits: Specifically, the corrective actions taken led directly to the low-inflation, high-growth environment of the mid-1980s through the late 1990s. In fact, since the WIN era, we

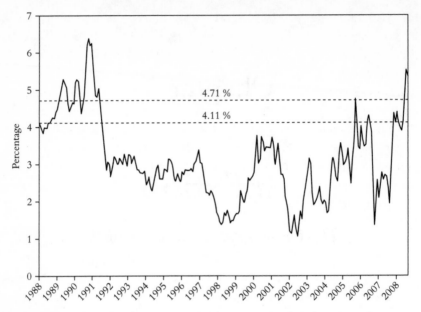

Figure 3.1 Inflation (Measured by the Consumer Price Index) Over the
Past Two Decades
SOURCE: U.S. Bureau of Labor Statistics.

have seen a multidecade period of declining interest rates and benign
inflation.

Many structural changes to the economy have taken place in the
past few decades to help keep inflation in check: tighter controls on
monetary policy and the ability to react faster; outsourcing, which
keeps wage costs under control; inventory management systems that
smooth out supply and demand imbalances; and a more global economy that can export inflation and competes for capital and labor.

At the beginning of 2008, it appeared the long-term downward
trend of below-average inflation was coming to an end. Over the past
two decades inflation has remained in a range of roughly 2 to 3 percent
(as shown in Figure 3.1), for an average of 3.06 percent. This is below
the 50-year average of 4.1 percent, and the 40-year average of 4.71
percent.

With a liquidity bubble in full throttle and asset prices accelerat-
ing along with wages, it had appeared the trend was going to change:
Excess liquidity pumped into the system after the tech bubble and

recession of earlier this decade and the funding of the war would work its way into the economy…finally. All that changed, however, during the summer of 2008, when massive deleveraging began as assets were sold to raise cash and meet liquidity needs. It was the world's largest margin call as the subprime mess and mark-to-market accounting rules on subprime loans held on books created a liquidity squeeze.

The problem began when home prices declined and securities tied to the debt of these assets plummeted. Banks, investment banks, pension funds, and investment funds scrambled to raise cash. Long-term liabilities had been funded with short-term debt, but then there was no more short-term debt. Cash had to be raised by selling assets. Deleveraging caused a massive decline in everything from gold and soybeans to oil and stocks. With limited credit available, home prices continued to decline. Deflation quickly became the concern.

The Consumer Price Index (CPI) for August 2008 dropped by 0.4 percent (before seasonal adjustment), as commodities depreciated by 30 to 50 percent, unemployment ticked up to more than 6 percent, and stock prices declined to levels not seen since earlier this decade. While this will change the short-term outlook on inflation, it is clear that all the rescue and bailout packages will result in more—more bond, more money supply, more debt, and more taxes. While this should be a drag on the economy, it will ultimately and hopefully be inflationary.

Inflation to the Rescue

The only way to solve the current problems will be to reinflate these assets, and to pay back debt with cheaper dollars. So while the inflation spiral was thwarted by a massive deleveraging of assets and a contraction of debt along with a slowing economy, the cure will be a resumption of inflation engineered by the Treasury's bailout package. So inflation is coming—not just as soon as it originally appeared.

As a consequence of all the bailout measures, we will eventually enter a long-term, upwardly sloping inflation trend. I am not saying that it will look like the bell bottom and punk rock era all over again, but compared to what we experienced in the past few decades, it may very well feel like we're revisiting 1980. After a period of deflation due to deleveraging, inflation will begin to perk up. It will sneak up on us because the liquidity crisis has been overpowering the headlines. There will be hints that at the end of the bailout rainbow inflation is waiting (and it's wearing a green suit and holding a four-leaf clover). After all, these assets sitting on the government's or its appointee's balance sheets need to appreciate.

Remember, inflation is not always a bad thing for investors. Even in an inflationary environment there are opportunities for the investor. In fact, some inflation is necessary to create wealth by owning assets. One of the most important lessons is managing your personal balance sheet.

Among the strategies that we'll discuss here and in later chapters is managing debt that can be paid back with "cheaper" dollars—specifically borrowing to purchase appreciating assets is a perfect example. Ideally, what you borrow should be a depreciating asset, thus creating depreciating liability; a perfect example is money during an inflationary period. In an inflationary environment, the dollars you borrow today are worth less tomorrow, so they are, in fact depreciating. Now take that depreciating asset (money) and purchase an appreciating asset. As we've seen, equities and real estate (the present bubble burst notwithstanding) have been positively sloped over time.

Causes of Inflation

Inflation, as we well know, is the result of too many dollars chasing too few goods. While that's true, there are many other factors contributing to the degree to which inflation becomes an issue. Typically, easy money and higher wages are the main culprits needed to start an inflation spiral. Or, as Milton Friedman, the Nobel Prize-winning economist told us, inflation is a monetary phenomenon caused by an increase in money. However, as we've seen in the recent past, there are times when we can have either one or both of those elements present in the economy without inflation becoming a worry.

For example, as Figure 3.2 shows, money supply growth since 2000 did not lead to a correlating increase in the CPI, a key inflation indicator. Focusing on the time period of 2000 through 2002 in particular, while money supply (M2) spiked higher, CPI actually trended lower.

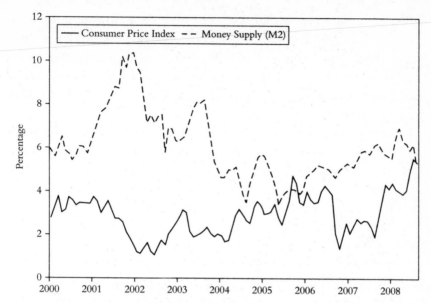

Figure 3.2 Despite Spikes in Money Supply (M2), Inflation Remained Comparatively Low
SOURCE: Federal Reserve; U.S. Bureau of Labor Statistics.

Similarly, there have been periods of wage growth in which there was not a correlating rise in inflation. As illustrated in Figure 3.3, rises in median weekly earnings in 1986, 1992, and 1998 actually coincided with periods of declining CPI. The reason for this seemingly contradictory phenomenon was that productivity gains and outsourcing of labor helped employers to offset rising wages. Additionally, real wages are calculated by subtracting overall CPI (not core) from wages. Therefore, if wages increase at the rate of the core (e.g., June 2008 report core was up 0.3 percent) but the overall CPI was up much greater (up 1.1 percent in June 2008), real wages are said to have gone down. (In June 2008, real wages were reported to have declined by 0.8 percent based on the equation: 0.3 percent − 1.1 percent = −0.8 percent.) Thus, when wages are calculated during periods in which there is higher overall CPI than core CPI, unless the overall number falls back in line with core, wages will appear to have gone down.

Looking at this further, we can see that the decade of the 1990s was a time of steadily rising industrial production (see Figure 3.4). Increases in output and efficiencies helped employers to meet increasing demand,

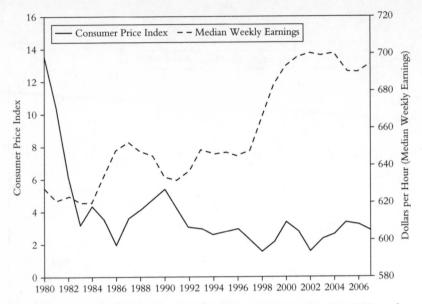

Figure 3.3 Inflation (CPI) Remained under Control During the 1990s and
Early 2000s, Despite Periods of Rising Median Wages
SOURCE: U.S. Bureau of Labor Statistics.

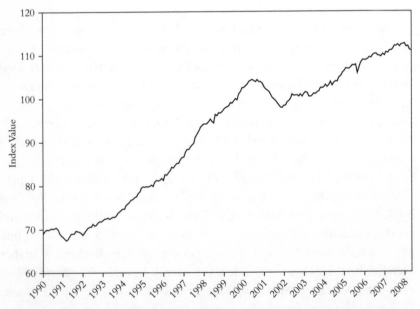

Figure 3.4 Industrial Production Rose through the 1990s and Remained at
Higher Levels in the 2000s
SOURCE: Federal Reserve Board.

60

especially consumers' appetites for the latest technology and gadgets, without having to increase prices.

The Wage-Inflation Equation

While higher wages are often a catalyst sparking inflation, their impact has been offset by other factors, specifically outsourcing of jobs to lower-cost countries. Outsourcing (or "offshoring," as this practice is also called) helped employers to take advantage of global wages, which remain low. The domestic U.S. workforce retained higher-wage jobs, but companies' overall labor costs benefited from the exporting of jobs.

According to a Bureau of Labor Statistics (BLS) study, in the early 1990s labor productivity, measured as output per hour, began to grow at a faster rate than had been seen in the previous 17 years. Although this would be expected with the economic recovery that was occurring at the time, what was unusual were productivity gains that accelerated even further in the mid- to late-1990s. The pace of productivity growth normally would be expected to slow as recovery matured.

An economic slowdown/recession did result in a slowing of labor productivity growth in 2001, compared to the previous five years, but it was still expanding at a quicker pace than in previous recessions. The BLS report noted, "...Coming out of the 2001 recession, business sector productivity growth advanced at its fastest rate since 1950 and maintained its rapid rate during 2003, including the dramatic 9.4 percent annual growth rate reported for the third quarter." [1]

Outsourcing jobs, the BLS report stated, did not affect productivity in the United States. Rather, it changed the mix of how and where companies produced goods (or components that went into finished goods) and provided services. As lower-compensated jobs were exported to take advantage of cheaper labor overseas, higher salaries paid in the United States were offset. However, because the higher wage earning jobs remained onshore, the average wage actually increased—even though wage costs to producers remained the same or lower. In fact, as Figure 3.5 shows, unit production costs increased at a much slower rate than CPI, reflecting the benefits of offsetting higher wages.

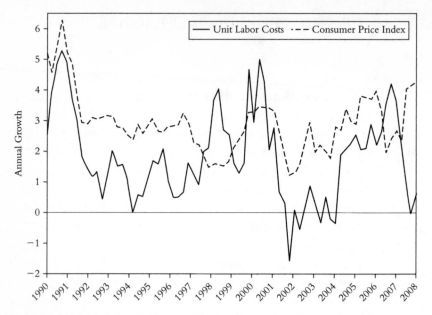

Figure 3.5 Unit Labor Cost Increases Grew at a Slower Pace than CPI
SOURCE: U.S. Bureau of Labor Statistics.

Additionally, companies benefited from the savings that resulted as production and inventory systems became much more efficient. Producers were able to keep up with demand and the need for price increases to get back to equilibrium; therefore, a reduction in demand was not needed. In other words, at current prices producers were able to meet increased demand. As a result, inflation was kept in check for most of the decade.

I remember reading an article several years ago in which a manufacturer of t-shirts and apparel defended his company's practice of outsourcing labor. If not, he said, a t-shirt would cost something like $90. On a trip to Target soon thereafter I found my favorite t-shirts on sale—not one, but three for $15. They were so "cheap" I bought them in every color: crewneck, v-neck, with a pocket, without a pocket. Did I really need two dozen t-shirts? No, but because the price was so low—seemingly *artificially* low given the value I placed on them (and more on this discussion later in the chapter)—I was enticed to buy more.

Consumers buying more increases demand; manufacturers meeting demand without raising prices keeps inflation in check. The way this occurs is by controlling wage costs.

Wage Pressures and Inflation

While outsourcing has helped to offset rising domestic wages, it's important to understand the more traditional relationship between wage pressures and inflation. To illustrate, let's assume the economy has two workers—Ken and Roz—each earning $100. Further, in this fictional economy, there are only two goods, guns and butter. The highest price a gun or butter could fetch is $200 (if Ken and Roz pooled their assets). The only way for the price of both goods to go up is for either Ken or Roz to earn more money. If this occurs with money growth (thereby creating the classic inflation scenario of more money chasing fewer goods), the result is inflation.

Supply and demand shocks that impact the price levels of needed goods (like gasoline today) generally push wages higher as people go to their employers and ask for more money. During the past few decades, however, workers were hesitant to ask for raises and, instead, tapped into their equity accounts or 401(k) savings. A rising stock market through the 1990s offset consumers' concerns about capital. At the same time, companies exporting wage pressures at most levels by outsourcing jobs to developing countries with cheaper labor allowed inflation to remain in check.

As late as the second quarter of 2008, in spite of the economic weakness, the labor market remained relatively tight as the growth in total nonfarm employment illustrated (see Figure 3.6). It appears that a tight labor market and the reemergence of inflation would most likely result in increases in labor costs. The reason? Workers would seek higher pay because of increased costs of things such as gasoline and food. However, an economic recession—the classic cure for inflation—defused the situation.

With a tight labor market, the cycle of higher prices and higher wages becomes a bit of chicken-and-the-egg; what came first depends upon how you look at it. Clearly, when employers are paying more in wages there comes a point when these increased labor costs must be passed along in the form of higher prices paid by their customers. If the customers are other businesses, then those price increases are passed along down the line, ultimately to the end user or consumer, who, facing higher prices, will seek higher wages.

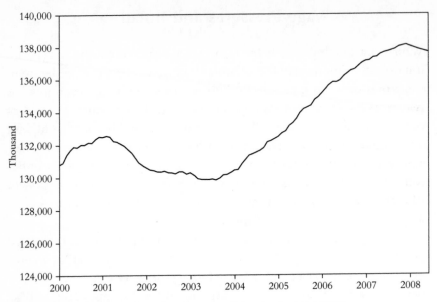

Figure 3.6 Total Nonfarm Employment Rises in the Mid-2000s
SOURCE: U.S. Bureau of Labor Statistics.

In the days of large bargaining agreements for the manufacturing sector, we saw the impact of higher cost-of-living adjustments (COLA) on wages and, therefore, employers' costs. For example, a 1981 analysis of COLA and higher wages by the Bureau of Labor Statistics examined the size of wage increases to reflect higher living costs. As the report noted at the time:

> Fifty-seven percent of workers covered by major agreements have cost-of-living protection. COLA clauses are designed to help workers recover purchasing power lost through price increases… While deferred wage changes affect the largest portion of workers, cost-of-living increases may be larger than deferred increases in 1981. If inflation continues as it did during 1979 and in 1980, COLA payments are likely to have a significant impact on the total wage changes occurring during the year. More than four-fifths of workers with COLA clauses will have at least one review during 1981. . . .[2]

With the change in the labor market, as manufacturing jobs become a smaller percentage, labor contracts for the autoworkers or mineworkers have less of an economic impact. When the economy recovers, we will likely see higher labor costs in the future, which will add to the expected inflationary pressures.

Keep in mind, too, that as other nations—particularly those that have benefited from the American business practice of outsourcing jobs— become more developed, workers in those countries will demand higher wages. The cost of goods in those markets will also go up, and inflation will edge higher, as well. The impact of even a minor increase in wages in foreign labor markets will cause an exponential increase for American companies in the cost of producing goods. This will eventually impact the American economy, causing inflation and, as a result, higher wages domestically. And when this happens, you should be prepared.

Oil Prices: The Ouch That Stings

Early in 2008, when asked about inflation, the average person's very first thought would be energy—not labor costs. Even those who were not directly hit felt the impact in their business or some related part of their lives. Now, at the risk of being the devil's advocate here, I would like to offer another point of view. It was payback time.

Over the past 10 years or so, consumers purchased large, gas guzzling SUVs and flew to tourist destinations like Florida, California, and Las Vegas for $99 bucks. We consumed and consumed, and yet airlines and other businesses went bust because they did not pass along price increases to consumers. The prices of many goods and services were kept artificially low for so many years even as demand increased.

Essentially, the output of a unit of energy that the consumer purchased was yielding more "bang for the buck." Since larger vehicles could haul more passengers and cargo (like groceries) then, theoretically at least, they offered the perceived economy of making fewer trips. A very realistic example is the road trip with two families. Rather than taking two cars (twice the gasoline, twice the wear-and-tear on the vehicle), everybody can pile into the monster SUV.

On a bigger scale, when airlines loaded up their planes with business travelers, tourists, and leisure travelers who were going somewhere just because the airfare was so cheap, it could be achieved for a few cents per mile. And this was occurring while oil prices were steadily rising.

Prices could only be kept lower than market forces would dictate for so long before something happened. One of those occurrences, as we've seen with airlines cutting back on flights and some carriers going out of business, is reduced supply. Another impact of higher energy prices was the cost of an airline ticket. The sticker shock we experienced at the gas pump also surfaced when looking at the price of what used to be a $100 or $200 airfare, which was hiked to $400 or more.

While consumers were aggravated, what they fail to recognize, however, was that the cost of airfares in the past were artificially low because of competition. Even when airlines faced higher costs, including for energy, airfares were kept relatively low. Airlines and related businesses subsidized the cost of transportation because they thought market share was more important than profit. The cost-pressure built to the point that something had to give—and that was the price of a round-trip ticket to just about anywhere. This explained why producer prices rose more than consumer prices, thus impacting the inflation rate and, more importantly, investors' views of inflation at the time.

While the price of energy increased and at a pace that couldn't be explained by simple short-term supply and demand models, if you looked at the context of a longer time period, you would understand that we had reached a tipping point where even a small change in supply with no reduction in demand caused exaggerated price swings.

Inflation Is Always an Issue

From a purely economic standpoint, inflation is *always* an issue. It may be that economic conditions at a particular point in time are not inflationary, but that doesn't mean inflation is any less important. Although there have been periods of deflation during our country's history, it is a rarity. If left unchecked, deflation can be even more destructive than inflation as it is more difficult to get the deflation genie back in the bottle. A common misnomer most economists, journalists, and investors use is actually referring to disinflation, which is lower levels of inflation. The culprit we're talking about post-credit bubble is deflation.

Table 3.1 Historical Inflation Rate from 1970–2007, from a High of 13.5 Percent in 1980 to a Low of 1.55 Percent in 1998

2007	2.86	1988	4.10
2006	3.23	1987	3.58
2005	3.37	1986	1.94
2004	2.67	1985	3.53
2003	2.30	1984	4.37
2002	1.60	1983	3.16
2001	2.82	1982	6.16
2000	3.37	1981	10.38
1999	2.19	1980	13.50
1998	1.55	1979	11.25
1997	2.34	1978	7.63
1996	2.94	1977	6.47
1995	2.81	1976	5.77
1994	2.60	1975	9.14
1993	2.97	1974	11.01
1992	3.04	1973	6.26
1991	4.22	1972	3.28
1990	5.42	1971	4.23
1989	4.79	1970	5.88

The Federal Reserve, with its mandate of promoting employment and noninflationary growth, closely watches inflation. It's always on the radar screen, even when it doesn't appear to be moving.

Looking at Table 3.1, we can see that inflation has ranged from a low of 1.55 percent in 1998 to a high of 13.58 percent in 1980.

While the contrast is stunning, the facts remain that: (1) there is always some degree of inflation; and (2) it is always addressed in every time period by the Federal Reserve, as we will examine through four decades and the chairmanship of three leaders.

The 1970s: Whipping Double-Digit Inflation

Federal Reserve Chairman Paul Volcker could have been known as the man who put the United States in a "double-dip" recession in the early 1980s. Instead, his legacy is far more positive: He's the one who executed monetary policies that tamed runaway inflation. As Table 3.1 shows, the year Volcker took the reins inflation was hitting double-digits, a lofty level that would persist through 1981, finally returning to single digits (but still comparatively high) in 1982.

The hallmark of the Volcker years was the legendary anti-inflation battle with bold—if unpopular—moves to save the economy. As Volcker stated in a recent PBS interview reflecting on that period of time, "I certainly thought that inflation was a dragon that was eating at our innards, or more than our innards, and if anybody was going to deal with this it was going to have to be the Federal Reserve. . . ."[3]

In a speech commenting on 25 years of monetary policy, former Federal Reserve Chairman Alan Greenspan saluted Volcker's leadership, as he described the 1970s as a time when "the ugly reality of stagflation forced an overhaul of this policy framework. The corrosive influence of inflation on our nation's productive potential was beginning to take hold."

On October 6, 1979, the Fed took "decisive action," Greenspan observed, to address the nation's need to battle inflation head-on. On that day, the Fed adopted new policy procedures that led to double-digit interest rates and two recessions, but that also successfully combated inflation and is credited with ushering in nearly two decades of low inflation and general economic stability.

Throwing the economy into recession not once but twice was strong medicine, but the overall health of the system was at stake. Looking back on the Fed's actions in October 1979, Greenspan remarked, "We owe a tremendous debt of gratitude to Chairman Volcker and to the Federal Open Market Committee for their leadership and steadfastness on that important occasion and for restoring the public's faith in our nation's currency."[4]

The Greenspan Years

By the time Greenspan became chairman of the Federal Reserve in 1987, the major economic issue was maintaining stability. Greenspan did earn his stripes quickly in the 1987 stock market "crash," or Black Monday, as it's referred to (even though I contend it was a system failure, and not a real crash—see Chapter 2). He responded by immediately

providing liquidity and lowered rates as well, which made credit available
to the brokerage and clearing community to ensure the clearing process
would remain solvent. It was just a few days prior that Greenspan's first
action at the Fed was to raise rates in an attempt to slow the economy
and support the dollar. The immediate about-face earned Greenspan the
respect of the market and taught him a lesson he practiced throughout
his tenure; that was, adding liquidity can solve any problem.

Indeed, by comparison, (including the 1987 "crash") Greenspan's
long run as Fed chairman would be less difficult than Volcker's war waged
on inflation. Nonetheless, Greenspan would face his challenges, from the
"irrational exuberance" (one of the best-remembered Greenspan-isms)
of the stock market to the Long Term Capital Management debacle that
set up a scenario in which the Federal Reserve would have to orchestrate a bailout of an overleveraged hedge fund whose demise was seen as
threatening the stability of the entire financial system.

Over his nearly two decades at the helm of the Fed, however,
Greenspan would have Volcker to thank. Without his predecessor's
tough actions to keep inflation under control, Greenspan would have
faced far different challenges.

Interestingly, while inflation appeared dormant, particularly in the
mid- to late-1990s, the Fed remained watchful. In testimony before
Congress in February 1997, Greenspan emphasized the need to continue the course of keeping inflation contained.

He called the low inflation of 1996 a "symptom and a cause" of a
good economy, with solid expansion minus major strains on resources.
Low levels of inflation and inflation expectation have helped to create a
positive financial and economic environment supportive of strong capital spending and longer-range planning—which also helped to sustain
an expanding economy.

Greenspan did not declare inflation dead or even a nonissue. Clearly,
the Federal Open Market Committee (FOMC) had its eye on inflation,
even at low levels. "Looking ahead, the members of the FOMC expect
inflation to remain low and the economy to grow appreciably further.
However . . . the unusually good inflation performance of recent years
seems to owe in large part to some temporary factors, of uncertain lon-
gevity," Greenspan told the Senate Committee on Banking, Housing,
and Urban Affairs in 1997. "Thus, the FOMC continues to see the

distribution of inflation risks skewed to the upside and must remain especially alert to the possible emergence of imbalances in financial and product markets that ultimately could endanger the maintenance of the low-inflation environment. Sustainable economic expansion for 1997 and beyond depends on it."[5]

By 2003, after the United States had concluded military operations in Iraq for the Gulf War, Greenspan's inflation concerns were about disinflation. In testimony before the House Committee on Financial Services in July 2003, Greenspan noted: "In the months since [April 2003], some of the residual war-related uncertainties have abated further and financial conditions have turned decidedly more accommodative, supported, in part, by the Federal Reserve's commitment to foster sustainable growth and to guard against a substantial further disinflation."

He further noted in his testimony that, "The FOMC stands prepared to maintain a highly accommodative stance of policy for as long as needed to promote satisfactory economic performance. In the judgment of the Committee, policy accommodation aimed at raising the growth of output, boosting the utilization of resources, and warding off unwelcome disinflation can be maintained for a considerable period without ultimately stoking inflationary pressures."[6]

Bernanke Takes Over

After 18 years at the helm of the Fed, Greenspan stepped down as chairman in January 2006. In October 2005, President George W. Bush announced the appointment of Ben Bernanke as his successor. Bernanke, a Harvard graduate with a doctorate in economics from the Massachusetts Institute of Technology, had been chairman of Princeton's Economics Department, founding director of Princeton's Bendheim Center for Finance, and founding editor of the *International Journal of Central Banking*. Now all eyes were on Bernanke as he took over, dealing with an array of economic problems: a potential inflation spiral, an economic slowdown/recession, and—of course—the credit crisis.

Focusing on inflation, we zero in on Bernanke's Semiannual Monetary Policy Report to Congress, given in July 2008 before the

Senate Committee on Banking, Housing, and Urban Affairs. He voiced heightened concern over inflation, in particular rising oil and agricultural commodity prices, the effects of which were evident in retail prices for energy and food. The Fed chairman modified any sound of alarm by noting that, thus far, there had been limited impact on non-energy and nonfood finished goods and services.

An inflation threat remained, however, as businesses face persistently higher energy and raw materials costs, as well as increased prices for imported goods and materials due to the declining value of the dollar. These pressures could result in businesses passing on higher costs to their customers "more aggressively than they have so far," Bernanke said.

Of particular interest was the Fed Chairman's longer-term outlook, as he focused on the impact of higher inflation—or even the perception of persistently higher inflation—on consumers. Bernanke told Congress that FOMC policymakers have increased their forecasts for inflation in 2008 as a whole, although inflation was expected to be moderate in 2009 and 2010 due to slower global growth.

"However, in light of the persistent escalation of commodity prices in recent quarters, FOMC participants viewed the inflation outlook as unusually uncertain and cited the possibility that commodity prices will continue to rise as an important risk to the inflation forecast," he added. "Moreover, the currently high level of inflation, if sustained might lead the public to revise up its expectations for longer-term inflation."

And if that happens? Here Bernanke pointed to the formula for an inflation spiral: higher wages sparked by the need for consumers to earn more to pay for goods and services that carry bigger price tags. Or as he put it, "If that were to occur, and those revised expectations were to become embedded in the domestic wage- and price-setting process, we could see an unwelcome rise in actual inflation over the longer-term. A critical responsibility of monetary policy makers is to prevent that process from taking hold."[7]

If this potentiality becomes reality, we will see Bernanke take on yet another interesting job: inflation manager. After a period of deflation, some inflation will be needed to reinflate the value of assets. Rather than fighting inflation, Bernanke may have to manage it instead.

The Bull Inside the Bear: Your Inflation Opportunities

Just as the Fed uses the tools it has available to stimulate a slowing economy and control inflation, businesses and consumers also have options as to how they can respond. The way of doing business will certainly change in some sectors given the current inflationary conditions. One example is getting away from the just-in-time concept of inventory management touted in previous decades.

The main benefits of the technology revolution were productivity gains and inventory controls, which made the business cycle smoother as companies controlled inventory up to the minute, or "just in time." In fact, when you buy an item, a computer system automatically monitors the purchase, tries to replace the inventory, and estimates the amount of sales. During periods of low inflation, this has been a terrific development for businesses to be more efficient.

During inflationary periods, however, a little inventory accumulation is good; for example, having fuel supplies secured for extended periods of time or buying commodities such as corn or steel before prices escalate even further. These are the same challenges and opportunities that businesses confronted in the 1970s and early 1980s. At that time, my father, who was an executive at a steel fabricating company, bought large quantities of steel to stockpile in the face of escalating prices. His inventory management—which was the exact opposite of just-in-time—was meant to be a kind of hedge against higher prices. Yet his actions actually reaped a business opportunity. Some of the steel he bought in advance of even higher prices and then warehoused was not made into tubing and other fabricated products. Instead, his company sold some steel inventory to other manufacturers at the prevailing market price. He made a nice profit, without having to shoulder the fabrication costs—and all because he had the foresight to buy ahead in an inflationary environment.

In the future as companies face the same kinds of inflationary environment, particularly for energy, inventory management will become critical: how much to buy, when to buy, and how to hedge against price fluctuations.

Consumers, too, have opportunities to tap into an inflationary environment. One area is debt. While one should never be overleveraged so that making payments becomes problematic, if you are going to carry higher levels of debt the time to do it is during inflationary periods. You can borrow today and pay back with dollars tomorrow that, because of inflation, are worth less.

Similarly in an inflationary environment, as an investor, it's important to look for opportunities among companies that stand to benefit from an inflation: for example, those companies that have stockpiled raw materials inventories, a fact that you may discover by reading the business press or by examining a company's annual report. Also companies that have higher levels of debt (or leverage) on their balance sheets may be treated more favorably. This is a departure from the traditional investment approach of shying away from companies that have debt. Companies with some debt will be better off during inflationary periods (and ideally after or toward the end of the inflationary periods) than companies that hoard cash, do not build inventories, and are actually owed money from clients or customers. Those receivables, after all, will be paid with dollars that are less valuable in the future. As interest rates go up during inflationary periods, debt that is locked in at a lower interest rate is actually a competitive edge. Of course it should be noted that debt levels must stay within cash flow objectives and be serviced from normal business operations. The ability to pay down the debt if needed should be highly probable. In other words, those who don't need it but have it and use it prudently will benefit (as usual).

There is another benefit of an inflationary period that relates to your cash management. While money is a depreciating asset during times of inflation, when prices go up you should be more discerning about how you spend it, thus creating a bigger base of capital to invest elsewhere, or even to help manage your debt. When prices are kept artificially low—remember my three-for-$15 t-shirts?—the typical consumer's response is to buy more. Often, that means more than necessary. When prices rise due to inflation, the consumer thinks twice about making that purchase. Do I really need two dozen t-shirts? Or, do I really need to spend a weekend in (name your location) just because the airfare is cheap? By thinking twice we reap benefits from our credit card balances to the environment (by not having to throw out stuff we didn't use in the first place).

Stay Alert and Nimble

The overarching theme of Part I of this book has been to look at recent decades and derive the economic lessons from each notable period. As we look at the economic conditions of the 1970s, 1980s, 1990s, and the 2000s, we see the need to be alert and nimble.

Staying alert simply means to pay attention to the economic conditions. Although the news headlines of the day may be distracting if they focus on a particular event, it's essential to be aware of the bigger economic picture. Is the economy expanding or contracting? Has a particular sector expanded too much, to the point of inflating a bubble?

Aware of the broad economic landscape, investors can make better choices, as we'll discuss specifically in Part III. This means staying nimble; not following the crowd to an overbought market or sector, and not becoming wedded to your favorite investment strategy, regardless of market and economic conditions.

To sum up Part I, we return to the question we raised in Chapter 1. Has the world really changed? The answer is yes—and no. Yes, conditions change and different events attract attention, both positive and negative. Even the credit crisis and the ensuing events of 2008—which, as I stated in Chapter 1—have caused significant changes—have not changed the economy forever. Yes, the credit crisis, the liquidity crunch that forced banks and investment houses to merge or go bankrupt, and the Treasury bailout plan have changed forever the face of the financial sector. And the Fed has been given more power and more control (for better or worse). But the economy and the capitalist democracy we all enjoy are here to stay.

What remains the same is the cyclical nature of the economy, and the need to stay alert and nimble. For now, the bull inside the inflation bear is to move out of fixed income assets and invest in sectors that will benefit from inflation, such as commodity-related sectors. And don't be afraid to buy stocks, as equities are more likely to be an inflation hedge than in the past.

Part II

WHAT DOES IT ALL MEAN FOR ME?

Chapter 4

The Credit Cycle

T he economy rolls through reoccurring stages like a sine wave: expansion to peak, contraction to trough, and back again. As explained in Chapter 1, these four stages have distinct characteristics: growth during the expansion, overextension at the peak, the decline during the contraction, and then a bottom being put in at the trough.

Looking at current conditions, as of this writing in late 2008, things aren't as clearly delineated as in the past in the overall economic cycle. Over the past eight years or so, the stock market has been flat. Economic growth, as measured by GDP has averaged 3 percent in the last five years. Unemployment has been rising lately, hitting 6.1 percent in August 2008, the highest level in nearly five years, as shown in Figure 4.1. (In October, unemployment rose further to 6.5%.)

Add to that inflation, which as explained in Chapter 3, will most likely become more of an issue even though we're undergoing a period of deflation across asset classes. The bailout of the financial sector that was engineered by the Treasury Department and the Federal

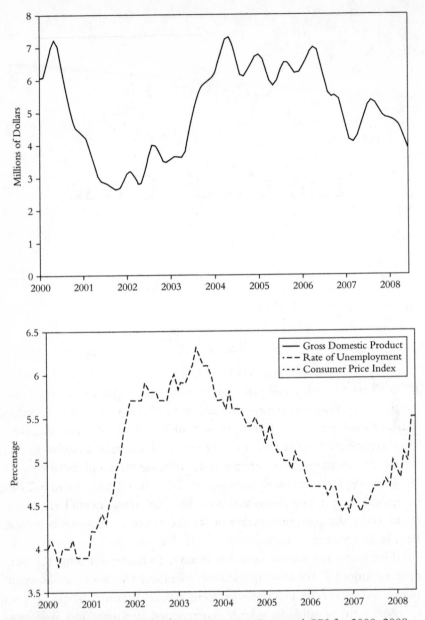

Figure 4.1 Snapshots of GDP, Unemployment Rate, and CPI for 2000–2008
SOURCE: U.S. Bureau of Labor Statistics; Federal Reserve Bank: Flow of Funds.

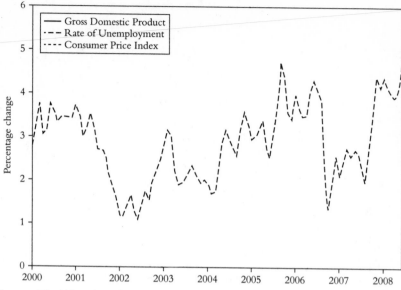

Figure 4.1 (Continued)

Reserve—and debated vigorously in Congress—will only put inflation on hold temporarily. This isn't going to stop inflation at all. Quite the contrary—as I'll explain later in this chapter, the Fed will need inflation to help reinflate the values of assets after a sharp decline.

First, we have to get through a period of deflation as deleveraging of assets takes place while credit tightens. Keep in mind inflation as I define it is not the result of higher energy and food costs. Although I've been backed into a corner a few times on this view, I'm sticking to my economic principles here. Inflation is excess money growth combined with higher wages.

That's my conundrum as an economist, to figure out what the current conditions mean from an inflation standpoint. Wages in the first half of 2008 were up 3.5 percent year-over-year, and money supply was up more than 10 percent. So while higher prices in energy and food captured consumer attention as well as headlines in early 2008, it was not the big story. That belonged to the credit market, which had clearly been in a contraction. The amount of available credit (Figure 4.2) decreased over the past 12 to 24 months as credit in the system was being pulled in.

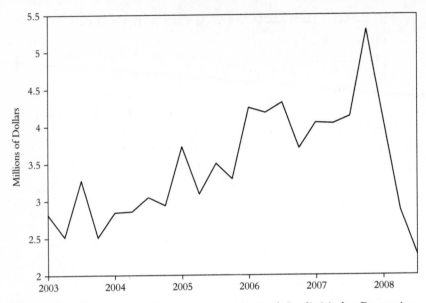

Figure 4.2   Credit Availability as Measured by Total Credit Market Borrowing
SOURCE: Federal Reserve Bank: Flow of Funds.

Rather than let the forces of nature run their course, however, the Treasury and the Fed have engineered a bailout for the financial sector that rivals anything we've seen in the past. If the market was stunned by the $29 billion in guarantees given to JPMorgan Chase in March 2008 to facilitate its takeover over Bear Stearns, that was only a warm-up for what was to come. Next was the initial AIG bailout to the tune of $85 billion in exchange for a majority stake in the firm. The real eye-popper, though, is the bailout of Wall Street that was initially estimated to cost $700 billion, and has well exceeded that.

This intervention has changed the dynamics of the credit cycle. The justification given by the government is that, without doing so, the financial sector was in danger of failing. Credit markets would seize up and the economy would come to a grinding halt. I maintain that the world would not have ended. It wouldn't have been pretty, but it was definitely not over. But there's no sense arguing what should have been done when that toothpaste is already out of the tube. Now we've got to discern, as best we can, what happens next and how we can prepare for it. But first, let's take a look at how we got here via the housing cycle.

An Overview of the Housing Cycle

An abundance of liquidity and easy credit terms helped fuel the expansion phase in housing. Housing prices expanded, particularly through the early 2000s, to hit a peak in 2006, followed by a decline in 2007 to 2008. As the Office of Federal Housing Enterprise Oversight (OFHEO) noted in its April 2008 report to Congress, as the housing sector weakened there was a sharp deceleration in house price appreciation in 2007, with downward pressure on property values from a large inventory of unsold homes.

The OFHEO's House Price Index (HPI) rose 0.8 percent and 0.5 percent, respectively, in the first two quarters of 2007, and then declined 0.3 percent in the third—the first drop in that index since the first quarter of 1993. The trend accelerated to the downside in the fourth quarter of 2007, with a 1.3 percent drop in the index. For 2007 as a whole, home values as defined by the OFHEO purchase-only index declined by 0.3 percent on average, compared with 4.1 percent growth in the year-ago period.[1]

The fall in prices accompanied a significant drop-off in home sales, which had kept up a brisk pace, particularly from the late 1990s into the early 2000s. Overall, home sales fell to levels not seen for several years. According to the OFHEO, single family housing starts declined by 29 percent in 2007 to 1.078 million units—the largest percentage decline on record and the lowest level of activity since 1992. Home sales also dropped sharply in 2007, with new home sales falling 26 percent to 776,000 units, the lowest volume since 1996. Existing home sales declined 13 percent to 5.7 million units, the lowest level since 2002.

The housing cycle continues to be in the contraction phase. This will be prolonged, with prices languishing at low (and even lower) levels until equilibrium is reached and buyers pick up their activity to push prices higher. The housing market, even while undergoing a cycle of its own, is really symptomatic of what's going on in the bigger picture: that is, the credit cycle. Housing suffered from classic overstimulation, overvaluation, and the easy credit conditions that caused it. The credit crisis is now working in a reverse spiral, sending the housing market into a recession. The spigot that flowed cash into anything collateralized by housing is essentially turned off.

The Four Phases of the Credit Cycle

The credit cycle—like the overall economy—goes through its own four phases of expansion, peak, contraction, and trough. Expansion was brought on by the low-interest rate environment maintained through much of the 1990s and 2000s. As previously explained—and alluded to in several places in the book—liquidity was pumped into the marketplace in response to other events (most notably the bursting of the tech bubble and as part of several rescue packages following September 11th). In time, it found its way into the credit market, sparking the housing boom along with other credit-related booms.

Given the amount of money available at attractive rates, borrowers from prospective homeowners to businesses were able to leverage up to buy assets. The more credit was available, the more borrowers came into the marketplace. Competition among lenders also increased as borrowers shopped for the best rates right down to the eighth of a percentage point.

Symptomatic of the latter phase of the expansion was overeagerness among lenders to extend credit to borrowers—including those with lower credit scores. Subprime and nontraditional mortgage lending rose from 2001 through 2006, which reflected a steady deterioration of underwriting standards.

The Pivotal Moment: A Nod to Minsky

The credit market went from expansion into a bubble in a pivotal moment marked by a shift in the dynamic between borrower and lender. Traditionally, a borrower approaches a loan officer at a bank or other lending institution with tax returns, bank statements, proof of employment, and the like in order to qualify for a loan. The borrower's plea is usually, "Please loan me money so I can buy that asset." As the credit market went from expansion to peak—and beyond that to a bubble—the borrower had all the bargaining power. Now it was the lender's turn to do the asking: "Please let me loan you money. You should borrow more so you can buy that asset."

This was the turning point, when the borrower was willing to become leveraged in order to buy an asset. The amount of leverage didn't matter to the borrower as long as prices continued to accelerate. Lenders didn't have to worry about defaults thanks to the securitization of loans that made them someone else's investment (read: problem). Even when a less qualified borrower came in, the question was still "how much do you want?" With less sophistication in home-buying, these borrowers were particularly vulnerable to buying more than they could afford.

Economist Hyman P. Minsky observed these pivotal moments in his theories of boom-and-bust cycles. When Minsky proposed his theories 25 years ago, they were not embraced—especially his call for the government to step in with more regulation to keep businesses and individuals from taking on too much risk. Minsky's theories are getting more of a serious look now, thanks to the credit crunch.

Minsky, a Harvard Ph.D., had five stages in his credit cycle model: displacement, boom, euphoria, profit taking, and panic. Displacement was caused as investors got excited about something; in this case, the availability of cheap and easy credit. This led to a real-estate boom, speculation in housing, and overvaluation. From the boom we transitioned to euphoria—that pivotal moment when instead of borrowers seeking out the lenders, the lenders were falling over each other to hand out money. The securitization of loans led to profits for speculators and investors during the euphoria. Then the smart ones began to take profits, which coincided with mid-2006. Then came the panic as the value of mortgage-backed securities collapsed.[2]

Minsky's five stages—displacement, boom, euphoria, profit taking, and panic—align well with the four-stages of the classic cycle. Displacement and boom encompass the expansion phase. Euphoria coincides with peak. Profit taking takes the market into contraction. Panic accelerates the contraction into the trough.

In the midst of the current contraction, we've seen more stringent lending policies, even for qualified borrowers, which will keep the credit market tight. I don't expect to see an easing until the bad loans are flushed out of the system and the lenders get healthier again. These conditions extend well beyond real estate and housing. Credit was extended for everything from cars, equipment, and airplanes to hedge funds and securities.

Emblematic of these times, perhaps, were the funds-of-funds-of-funds—or funds-of-funds-squared, as insiders called them. These were pools of hedge funds to which credit was extended in order to buy—yes, you guessed it—more hedge funds. The theory behind it was that diversification and risk management techniques would insulate capital from loss. Some of the funds-of-funds focused on asset-backed lending and credit swaps. They were actually buying loans and in some cases making loans, and once they reached a critical mass would take the loans to a bank to borrow more money against the loan portfolio in order to make more loans. And then they'd borrow more against those loans. Some funds did this 20 to 25 times, which sounds crazy until you realize that there were other players—Freddie Mac, Fannie Mae, and some banks—that actually did this hundreds of times, and would initiate a loan just to resell and borrow against.

If this sounds like the proverbial house of cards, you're right. And just as that image suggests, it did all come tumbling down. But rather than just let the market forces separate out the good, the bad, and the ugly, the government stepped in with a massive bailout to supposedly rescue the credit cycle from oblivion. I would argue, however, that tinkering with the cycle was akin to trying to fool Mother Nature. A much bigger problem can get created.

Banking 101

At the risk of providing an overly simplified example, let me give some perspective on what actually was happening and where the credit cycle went off the track. Let's say you deposit $1,000 in your bank. Your bank, in turn, is allowed to borrow against its deposits, either from the discount window or via Fed funds. Of that $1,000, the bank then loans out $500 to a widget company that accessed its line of credit, and $500 sits on its ledger. At the end of the day, someone at the bank sees how much is leftover based on the deposits taken in and the amount loaned out, and puts it into an overnight pool in order to make interest.

That overnight pool is accessed by other banks (as well as other borrowers). For example, a bank that loaned out $2,000 but only took in $1,000 in deposits needs to tap the funds overnight so that when a customer goes to the ATM, the money would be there. Maintaining the liquidity of the overnight pool is critical to keeping the system running. So what would happen if banks didn't want to put their money in the pool? While some banks may not have had the extra liquidity, there were more institutions that suddenly were concerned that they might not get the money back.

In order to improve their liquidity, banks turned to the Fed, which allowed parties to exchange certain assets—at first money-market instruments and short-term bonds—for overnight cash. The liquidity problems in the financial system worsened because of troubles at institutions, which were not federally chartered banks. These institutions were the other side of transactions with parties that participated in the overnight pool, thus affecting the entire system. In response, the Fed opened the swap window to more participants in order to keep the overnight pool going, which helped for a while.

Suddenly, things got to the point that securities were perceived to be worth "zero." Perhaps the security was a loan or a home mortgage backed by an asset that had dramatically declined in value or that had no real value. Loaning against assets with little or no value was impossible. Now what could the bank tell the depositor who wants to make a withdrawal? Sorry, but we don't have access to funding because we have a bunch of worthless assets on our books? Suddenly, there was the real possibility of a "run on the bank" as worried depositors yanked the money (a phenomenon we saw in money-market funds that had suddenly "broken the buck"—meaning a dollar invested was now worth $0.95 or $0.98).

The devaluation of the underlying assets—namely, real estate or securities tied to them—put everything into question. Suddenly the banks needed capital and consumers were afraid that, even though accounts are insured by the Federal Deposit Insurance Corporation (FDIC), they might not get their cash. Money markets were the first to be hit. Boston-based Putnam Investments closed a $12 billion money-market fund and returned investors' money after institutional clients pulled out cash, even though the fund did not have any exposure to troubled or at-risk assets.

The banking process has become far more sophisticated and complicated than just taking in money from depositors and loaning it out to home buyers and businesses. The securitization of debt—bundling loans and mortgages that are then sold off to investors—not only put the initial borrower and lender farther apart, it also increased the number of parties and counterparties that could be affected by a security. Now, when a home buyer defaults on a mortgage, it isn't the bank's concern. That loan was sold off as soon as the signatures on the documents were dry. But the pension fund that bought securitized debt to boost the return in its portfolio, or the hedge fund that bought the loan and then borrowed against it suddenly had to worry about not only the increase in defaults, but also the decline in the value of underlying assets.

Now enter mark-to-market accounting, which has created further havoc on bank's balance sheets. Here's the problem in a nutshell: While it's true that the default rate on loans—and subprime in particular— is higher, it's not like every loan that has been written is headed for default. Nonetheless, the fear over what *could* happen has pushed the value of these assets to rock-bottom levels—regardless of how these bonds actually perform. With mark-to-market accounting banks have had to value the assets on their books based on the market's perception that day, not actual performance or value of the security.

Brian Wesbury, chief economist of First Trust, illustrates the problem with mark-to-market accounting with this scenario: Imagine you had a $200,000 mortgage on a $300,000 house that you planned on living in for 20 years. Your neighbor, however, because of some special circum- stance had to sell his house for $150,000. Suddenly, your bank says that this "new market" is now the basis for the value of your house—and asks you for $80,000 in cash immediately so that you would have 20 percent down. What would the impact be? Chaos, of course.

As this scenario illustrates, mark-to-market accounting rules have cre- ated a great deal of turmoil in the financial sector. Repealing or amend- ing these rules, it seems, would be a far more expedient and less costly way to deal with the financial crisis than a bailout with a price tag in the hundreds of billions. Without mark-to-market accounting, banks would be able to clean up their balance sheets, meet their appropriate capital requirements, and function efficiently with more capital and less risk.

That is obviously not the route taken by the Treasury and the Fed, so arguing the merits of one approach or another is moot at this point. For the record, I will say that what has bothered me the most about the bailout, beyond the astronomical price tag, is the fact that it goes against free markets and pure capitalism. It used to be that if you made an investment that did well, you profited accordingly, and if it did poorly you lost money. And if the investment went bust, you lost your capital. This is the risk and reward that is inherent in capitalism in a democracy, which I wholeheartedly embrace.

Now, the government has changed the rules with a pattern of intervening that I believe sets a dangerous precedent. Rather than people and institutions learning their lesson by losing money and therefore being more risk-conscious in the future, they could conceivably adopt even riskier behavior, believing that the Fed will be there to bail them out. As for the government's argument that it will actually make money to offset the cost of the bailout, if that were true then count me in. I made the joke the other day that instead of paying my federal taxes this year, I'm going to contribute capital to the AIG bailout. If the government is going to make money by putting in $85 billion (and tens of billion more later on), then let me put in my share, too, in order to reap the return. Or if the $700 billion bailout means that my home, my business, and the school district in my community will benefit, then I'll gladly pay more than my share! What is unclear to me is how this capital is going to be deployed and to what end. If the outcome is not realized then we will have wasted an awful lot of money for a sub-par return.

To me, one has to weigh the impact of the turmoil in the financial sector on the entire U.S. economy, which is $13 trillion to $14 trillion. With no bailout, the economy would have stumbled and gotten a black eye, but I do not believe that all the money in the entire capital base in the nation would go away. Some assets would get marked down to zero and liquidity would freeze up. At the end of the day, people's money in the bank would not be at risk and companies would still make payroll. I'm not saying that it wouldn't be painful, as some assets would go to zero. Allowing market forces to work, to me, would be far better, especially in the long run.

Then, as previously discussed, I favor elimination of mark-to-market accounting in return for some other mechanism to create fair valuation of the assets, and also allow capital requirements to reflect the true value of the assets. This would create less of an impact from writedowns than we've seen throughout 2008.

I also have to ask whether investment banks that were publicly traded—such as Bear Stearns, Lehman Brothers, and Merrill Lynch—should have been set up differently. If they are going to be public, perhaps they need to be structured differently with restriction on shares and rules on shorting.

No matter how compelling the arguments to the contrary, the Treasury and the Fed have proceeded with their bailout. As of this writing, there is still much uncertainty. The long and short of it is we'll have to stay tuned and watch as this unfolds.

In the meantime, my advice to investors is that the extreme intervention measures undertaken by the government will set the stage for the next opportunity to capture the bull inside the bear. Even as the seeds of that expansion are planted, however, we will endure a severe contraction in several assets because of deleveraging.

Now the Deleveraging Begins

Contraction of the credit market has led to classic deleveraging. Assets are being sold at any price to cover debt. Virtually no asset is escaping the deleveraging. We've seen 30 to 50 percent declines in oil, gold, silver, corn, soybeans, and other commodities. If it can be sold for cash, it's being marked down with the bright red grease pencil and unloaded. It's like the used car dealership commercial: "no offer is too low." There's a fire sale going on and everything must go! If housing could sell as fast as everything else, it would be added to the list of slash-and-sell assets.

The downward pressure on asset prices is impacting the "faux" assets the hardest. These were the clever securities created to extend borrowing based on other securities as collateral, which weren't even saleable since they sit on the asset side of the balance sheet of many banks and investment houses. The monster that was created as an asset for the balance sheet is now ravaging the equity of these companies as liquidity becomes an issue, investor confidence is at a low, and stock prices have gotten pummeled by fearful investors. (For the record, the problem with the "short sellers" was much exaggerated, as short selling was only 2 percent of the market activity in financial stocks. The bigger pressure—as we saw after the Securities and Exchange Commission temporarily banned short selling in certain stocks—came from nervous investors who didn't want to put their capital at risk.)

Capitalization concerns resulted in a rush to get married, with investment banks with a good name and some equity left went off in search of a partner with a liquid balance sheet. China is a favorite partner these days as the government there is backed with funds that are flush with cash and U.S. government-backed securities.

The deleveraging spiral, however, is temporary. It is a market-triggered phenomenon that will, at some point, stop. In the background, we still have elevated levels of inflation, which complicates the picture. During inflationary times, the dollars you have today are worth less in the future. The typical strategy would be to use a depreciating asset (in this case dollars) to buy an appreciating one. As deleveraging becomes more widespread, just the opposite is happening. Although rates have dropped to levels never seen before, borrowing is almost impossible because who wants to loan against an asset in the midst of a deleveraging environment, when the asset could fall to less than the amount of the loan? In fact lenders (not necessarily banks) are trying to call in loans and reduce their exposure to assets they have loaned against.

Credit Cycle Impact

At my firm, Astor Asset Management, our calling card has been identifying and capitalizing upon the current stage of the economic cycle: expansion, peak, contraction, or trough. What we see happening in the credit market, however, goes beyond the normal flow of these cycles. Yes, it stings when the stock market drops 30 percent plus over several months, and you see double-digit percentage declines in your investment portfolio or your 401(k) account. Or when the house down the block sells for 20 percent less than you paid for a nearly identical house just last year.

It's an entirely different problem, however, when your money market account that has always traded at $1.00 is suddenly "below the buck" (meaning at $0.98 or $0.95, or some other amount), or worse yet you can't get to that money at all. Now you're less concerned about the return *on* your money and more worried about the return *of* your money. And that's the major difference between a contraction in credit and the impact on the economy and the financial system. When credit conditions contract so much that asset values fall below the nonleverage value, it's a serious concern. When your home is worth less than your mortgage, that's more than just a contraction in real estate/housing. It hurts everyone. Lenders have assets that they thought covered them and made them whole if the borrower defaulted. Instead, they are out actual dollars as well. If the problem should become widespread enough, then the money that a bank owes in deposits (which is a liability to the bank and an asset for the depositor) is in jeopardy. As the depositor you don't have any collateral. That is where the buck should stop, but how? With the government? If Uncle Sam is the backstop then why stop with depositor?

It all goes back to the formula for calculating the *unleveraged* value of an asset. An asset's value should not be determined by the ability to finance it. And if it is, then the value of many assets that cannot get financing should be zero. This underscores the point that credit cycles impact the value of other assets. This is not true with other cycles. For example, the bear market in stocks earlier in this decade did not impact the value of other assets, beyond the slowdown that was causing the bear market. In fact, housing enjoyed a continued expansion in value because of the credit market even while stocks languished. When credit crashed, it impacted the economy, housing, employment, and lastly the stock market.

The stock market took a beating as well, with the Dow down more than 40 percent as of November 2008. But remember other assets that are leveraged (stocks are generally not leveraged for the typical investor) are in far worse shape. A $500,000 house with a $400,000 mortgage that declines 15 percent is worth $350,000—less than the equity and a loss for the lender should it have to take the property over.

When money market funds invested in subprime notes, money that you thought was safe and secure is suddenly at risk and quite possibly gone. As I stated in Chapter 3, it's the world's largest margin call and some investors are not going to meet it.

The Bull Inside the Bear: It's Not the End of the World

Despite the shock waves hitting the credit cycle, it's not the end of the world. After the massive deleveraging in assets, which will swing well below fair value, the Fed and others will need to reinflate the economy.

Assets will increase in value at a pace that exceeds the normal trend of asset growth. This will create an opportunity to ride the bull in assets, stocks in particular. Importantly, these will be assets that can grow and appreciate without the help of credit and borrowing.

Of course, some degree of debt is necessary but not the amount of debt that will determine the value of assets contingent on financing. Once again, this points to equities. Equities are not debt. They are, well, equity. Companies that can grow without debt and have the ability later in the cycle to assume some debt will be in the best shape. This point of view supports value over growth. One investment possibility will be exchange traded fund (ETFs) that provide value exposure.

Cash will rule—and growth will lag.

One area of interest, as we'll explore later in the book, is exactly where all the trouble began: financials. The financial sector as a whole will not only survive but actually do quite well in time. Individual stocks will vary. But given the size and scope of the bailout, the entire sector has the full faith and guarantee of the U.S. government behind it. Rather than try to pick one or two financial stocks, a better strategy would be to get involved in the entire sector using an ETF like the XLF.

The point is a new bull market will surface after the credit crisis is resolved. That bull is in stocks, and the expansion that we're likely to see will be one of the strongest ones we've had in decades. It's not certain if the solution to the credit problem will be the rescue plan, or if it will occur because the economy and the business world in general will turn the corner of the current contraction. Whatever the cause, there is a bull inside this bear. So weather the storm in the credit market, and be prepared for better days ahead.

Chapter 5

The Housing Bubble

From Watch to Warning

W hen Herbert Hoover ran for president in 1928 he promised Americans, "A chicken in every pot and a car in every garage." Prosperity for all! If that sounds like "bubble talk," take a second look at the date. A year later would come the Crash of 1929, the classic bubble burst, and in the aftermath the United States was plunged into the Great Depression.

Now flash forward nearly 50 or 60 years to the thinking that took hold in the 1990s and grew through the decade of the 2000s, that just about everyone could be a homeowner. This appealed to deeply held beliefs from the adage that "a person's home is his/her castle." President George W. Bush seized upon this theme in his June 2002 remarks before the Department of Housing and Urban Development: "...I believe owning something is a part of the American Dream, as well. I believe when somebody owns their own home, they're realizing the American Dream," he said, and reiterated his goal of 5.5 million more homeowners by 2010.[1]

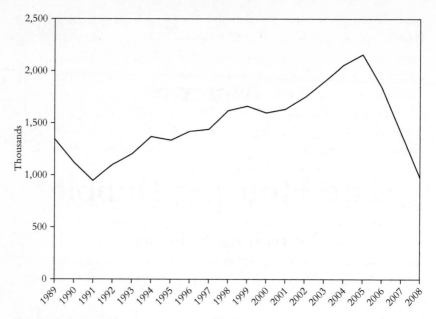

Figure 5.1   U.S. Housing Permits 1989–2008
Source: U.S. Census Bureau.

Sadly, for some homeowners the proverbial American Dream would turn into a nightmare, as the liquidity bubble burst, the expansion in the housing market came to an abrupt end and, by 2007, a million properties would be in foreclosure nationwide due to loan defaults.

Yet in the beginning, there were no real warning signs of the storm to come. Skies were clear and sunny, figuratively speaking. It was the perfect climate for building, as Figure 5.1 shows. Housing permits rose steadily through the 1990s and into the 2000s, fueling a housing market expansion.

Nearly 70 Percent Home Ownership in the United States

According to the U.S. Census Bureau, home ownership in the United States hit a high of 69.2 percent in the second quarter of 2004, compared with a recent low of 63.6 percent in the first quarter of 1986. A rise of nearly six percentage points in home ownership is statistically significant, given the size of the adult population in the United States. By first-quarter 2008, home ownership stood at 67.8 percent, which was on par with the fourth quarter of 2007, but down from over 68 percent earlier that year and as high as 69 percent in 2006. The bursting of the housing bubble was already showing up in slight erosion of home ownership percentages.[2]

If people viewed their homes as their castles, many also saw them as potential ATM machines. Higher home values meant more home equity. Home equity translated into an asset that could be tapped—meaning converted into cash through a home equity loan.

The size of home equity—calculated as the value of the home minus the mortgage principal—became the largest share of household net worth through the decades of the 1990s and 2000s, the Census Bureau also reported. Home equity accounted for 41.7 percent of household net worth in 2002 (the most recent year available in the report released in April 2008). Further, with 67.7 percent of households reported owning homes in 2002, median equity was $73,697—up from $63,278 in 2000. These findings partly reflect the beginning of the upturn in national housing values, and the overall decline at the time of the stock market from 2000 to 2002.[3]

Nesting Instinct

Beyond the numbers, there were other forces at work—societal and behavioral—that put greater emphasis on housing. From single people buying lofts and condos, to young couples with babies looking to sell their first home for a bigger one in the suburbs, to Boomers looking for a vacation home that would become their retirement oasis one day, a nesting instinct was taking hold.

From an economic perspective, what was happening was a shift in assets. Liquidity that was pumped into the system after the technology stock bubble burst of 1999 and 2000, and in the wake of the terrorist attacks of September 11, 2001, found its way into housing. This was hugely helped by low interest rates meant to spur the economy through a rough patch. While in the past decade liquidity would find its way into the stock market, this time around many investors had sworn off their stock buying binges. They learned that there was more to investing and building a portfolio than buying a dot-com (especially one with no earnings and not much in the way of revenues, either) and waiting for the price to go up. Investors had experienced the pain that what goes up also comes down; or perhaps better stated, what inflates into a bubble will eventually burst.

With the downturn in the stock market, investors took their toys and went home—literally. Interestingly, having experienced the inflating and bursting of one bubble—in tech stocks—they didn't recognize it occurring in another place, this time in housing. Banks were too busy lending including with new products such as an expanded use of adjustable rate mortgages (ARMs). In a low-rate environment, ARMs were extremely attractive to people who didn't want to "lock in" a rate, which they thought could go even lower.

Prospective homeowners busied themselves with buying, selling, remodeling, reselling, and moving. "Flipping" was no longer something to do with pancakes on a griddle, it was a well-known term among housing speculators who were not just professionals, but also regular folks on the block with liquidity to burn.

People not only wanted a home, but they wanted bigger and newer ones. "For sale" signs sprouted like dandelions on lawns and were quickly replaced with "sold!" notices. Neighbors who watched someone sell his or her house within weeks or even days—and at an elevated asking price—decided maybe they should give it a try. Why not get a bigger, newer, fancier house? As Figure 5.2 shows, the number of houses for sale were fairly stable through the late 1980s and early 1990s, before a huge surge took the number of houses for sale to new highs by the mid-2000s.

There were even cultural influences adding to the housing craze. There were entire cable television channels—HGTV (Home and Garden Television) and DIY (Do it Yourself)—devoted to home building, buying, and flipping. Ty Pennington—who, as explained later in this chapter, would also become a barometer of the mania—was a household name as the host of the program "Extreme Makeover: Home Edition."

But in the early days of the housing market expansion it seemed that, as Dorothy said so poignantly in the *Wizard of Oz*, "There's no place like home." No one worried about the expansion. Housing prices going up was a good thing. Higher home prices meant great asset values.

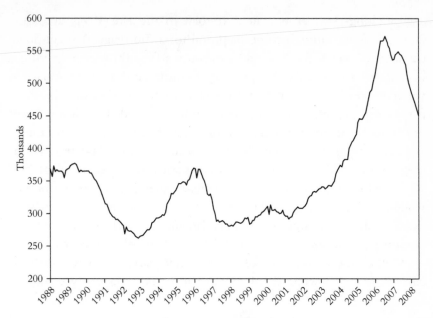

Figure 5.2 U.S. Single Family Houses for Sale 1988–2008
SOURCE: U.S. Census Bureau.

Empty-nesters who wanted to shed the four-bedroom house in suburbia could do so easily, cashing in on the equity that had grown rapidly in recent years. And it wasn't just young families who were moving in. The old paradigm of "get married, have a baby, buy a house" was changing. People chose the order that suited them, with the house (and sometimes the baby) coming before marriage. More and more single people owned their homes, whether houses or condos.

The housing market even looked different than it did 20 years before. Instead of the proverbial house with a picket fence, there were suddenly lofts and cool spaces with home theaters; kitchens that opened up to the living room. The "great room" was born. A drive outside just about any major city, through the suburbs, and all the way out to the "ex-burbs" showed farmland or vacant land turned into housing developments with appealing names. Why have just a house when you could own an "estate" in XYZ Manor?

All a wannabe-homesteader needed was a small down payment, maybe ten thousand or so from one's parents, and a job, even if there was no long-term employment history. In the late 1990s and early 2000s, that was enough to get approval for a mortgage. A small down payment of, say, $25,000 could get you a $150,000 mortgage with a loan-to-value of about 85 percent. In time, 100 percent financing would become more common, as well as a slew of other loan products from those that carried "teaser rates," which provided for lower initial payments, to others that increased the amount of principal over time.

Banks were happy to be lenders because of the low-rate environment and a yield curve that was not as positively sloped as in the past. With declining inflation and falling interest rates, banks were more than willing to loan money to borrowers with different credit qualities. As banks made loans, using homes as collateral, they increased the amount of mortgage and mortgage-related debt on their balance sheets.

Overall, the housing market was a happy place, complete with clear blue sky and puffy white clouds. But a change in the weather was coming.

The Weather Watch

Crying foul on the housing market expansion was like throwing eggs at the front porch. No one wanted to say that the expansion in housing prices was a bad thing. Homeowners liked it because they could sell for more than they bought, and homebuyers liked it because the appreciation of what they were buying seemed assured. And banks liked it because as they loaned to people with lower credit scores, the prospect of higher prices reduced the risk. If someone got behind in his or her payments, refinancing could pay off a mortgage and provide a cash cushion. Or, in the worst-case scenario, the bank would end up holding an appreciating asset.

Another comforting factor as housing prices rose is that household income kept pace, as Figure 5.3 shows. As incomes went up, people felt confident about "stretching" to buy a home that was outside their comfort zone. Realtors and bankers frequently gave prospective buyers the advice of buying bigger (or more expensive); after all, prices were going up.

There were early warning signs as a few dark clouds appeared in the blue skies of the housing market. Nothing was overtly wrong as yet, but enough concern had surfaced that the term "housing bubble" was

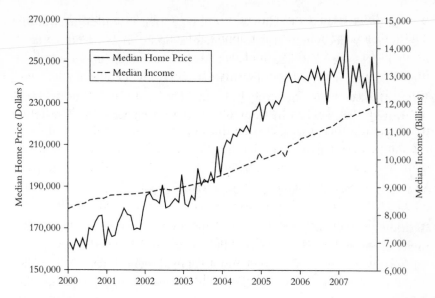

Figure 5.3   Median Income versus Median Home Prices, 2000–2008
SOURCE: Bureau of Economic Analysis; U.S. Census Bureau.

being spoken about even in the early 2000s. Many people, however, dismissed the worries with explanations of everything ranging from the belief that the housing market was too fragmented to experience a true bubble-and-burst to the idea that housing prices would keep escalating because of strong demand.

Even Federal Reserve Chairman Alan Greenspan, in testimony in April 2002 before Congress' Joint Economic Committee, wasn't sounding an alarm—as yet. "The ongoing strength in the housing market has raised concerns about the possible emergence of a bubble in home prices," he told Congress. "However, the analogy often made to the building and bursting of a stock price bubble is imperfect."

For one thing, housing transactions are different, involving substantial transaction costs and the need for people to move out of the property that they've sold, Greenspan reasoned. "Doing so often entails significant financial and emotional costs and is an obvious impediment to stimulating a bubble through speculative trading in homes. Thus, while stock market turnover is more than 100 percent annually, the turnover of home ownership is less than 10 percent annually—scarcely tinder for speculative conflagration."[4]

Greenspan also saw limited arbitrage opportunities in housing compared to securities. In his example, a home in Portland, Oregon, can't be swapped for one in Portland, Maine, which underscored his belief that the national housing market was really a collection of small, local markets. But when the housing bubble hit the liquidity crisis, it created a perfect storm from which no region was safe. The entire housing market—coast-to-coast—declined.

A Loan for Everyone

During the housing bubble, credit quality deteriorated, and lending practices—even at very reputable institutions—welcomed a new group of borrowers who under more normal circumstances wouldn't qualify. Now, it's important to understand that I'm *not* saying that broadening homeownership is a bad thing. Nor am I trying to exclude or discourage anyone who truly wants to pursue the proverbial American dream of owning his or her own home. However, putting on my dispassionate economist's hat, I have to question the viability of home ownership for people who never planned on owning and maintaining that asset in the first place. Just because it was possible to get a "no doc" loan (no documentation needed to prove income, assets, or other eligibility), doesn't make it the best thing for that particular person. When what looks like a gift becomes a harsh burden because it's way beyond someone's income stream, then it's just plain wrong to encourage homeownership for that individual.

As credit quality deteriorated so did the loan-to-price (also known as loan-to-value) ratio. As Figure 5.4 shows, by the late 1990s and early 2000s loan-to-price on a composite basis approached 80 percent, and when it declined in the early 2000s, it didn't fall all that far to the mid-70 percent.

Compounding the troubles in the credit market were folks who normally would have had pretty good credit, but had gotten themselves in over their heads. Stories abound of two-income families with a mortgage and a nice little growing nest egg of home equity who decided (or were enticed by advertising) to put that home value to work. So off they went to the local bank or other lending institution

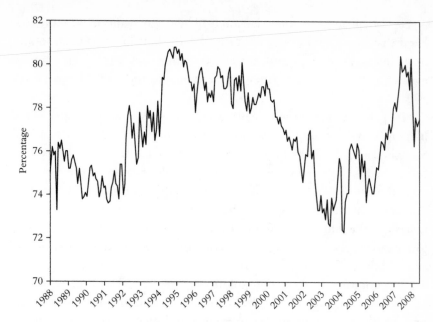

Figure 5.4   Composite Loan-to-Price Ratio 1988–2008
SOURCE: Federal Housing Finance Board.

to secure a home equity loan, which often had a floating rate. That may have been a great deal when mortgage rates were somewhere around 5 percent and interest on the home equity loan was just above 3 percent. As long as interest rates were low and housing prices went up, everything was fine.

But this was a house made of straw—not bricks, and a strong wind was about to send it tumbling down. A decline in housing prices coupled with the ratcheting up of interest rates put borrowers in a squeeze. They were paying more than they could afford, and if they tried to sell their homes, buyers had become scarcer. Moreover, if they sold, they faced the prospect of not covering the full amount of the principal owed for the mortgage and the home equity loan.

Some borrowers had also gotten themselves into trouble because the loans themselves were appreciating. As stated in Chapter 3, the "classic" investment approach is to utilize a depreciating asset (such as money during inflationary times) to buy an appreciating one (such as housing in the 1990s and in the early 2000s). Unfortunately, some homebuyers reversed that order to their detriment. They signed on for interest-only loans that never paid down the principal, or their loans were structured in such a way—such as with teaser rates—that they were paying for less over time. In other words, they owed more and more on a depreciating asset.

Negative amortization loans even increased the principal owed, helping people to buy "more home" than they could otherwise afford. Stretched to the maximum, they could take on a $500,000 loan to buy a $1 million house in a pricey locale. However, the home of their dreams was actually $1.2 million. So the mortgage was based on a $1 million purchase upfront, but over time the principal increased to reflect the full $1.2 million. Even with a good income, it was far too easy to get behind on payments, or to be stretched beyond all reasonability.

It's not that the creative solutions were "bad" in and of themselves. The financial market has thrived on innovation to help create opportunities for both risk management and speculative profit-making. Limiting the array of lending options isn't the objective of this discussion. Rather, lending options were taken by the wrong people, who either underestimated or misunderstood the risks involved. While it's easy to shake a finger of shame at the banks, borrowers have to shoulder their share.

As the credit crisis worsened, financial cushions that people could draw were becoming thinner and a little threadbare. As Figure 5.5 shows, the personal savings rate declined precipitously through the 1990s and into the 2000s, even going negative as people took on debt they could not afford.

By 2006, mortgage originations among less-than-prime borrowers were still climbing, including some $400 billion of midlevel or "Alt-A" loans—which are between prime and subprime, up from $85 billion in 2003, according to industry figures. Alt-A loans accounted for roughly 16 percent of mortgage originations in 2006 and subprime loans were an additional 24 percent, according to industry figures. The Alt-A category also included mortgages that carry little documentation of income or assets; option ARMs, which give borrowers multiple payment choices; and sometimes loans taken by investors buying homes they don't plan to occupy themselves.[5]

Figure 5.5   Personal Savings Rate 1988–2008
SOURCE: Bureau of Economic Analysis.

From Watch to Warning

The climate was definitely changing in the housing market. To use our weather analogy, the watch that had predicted the possibility of turbulent times had escalated into a warning that indicated a strong probability. Indeed, over time rising debt, lower savings, increased subprime lending, and falling housing prices made for a confluence of factors that would yield a perfect storm.

By 2004, Greenspan had changed his tone, from the cautionary watch that amounted to a chance of showers in some areas, to more of a warning, although he wasn't sending anyone for cover just yet. In remarks in October 2004 at a community bankers' annual convention, he stated, "... Many have recently become increasingly concerned about the exceptional run-up in home prices. They argue that a collapse of such prices would expose large, recently incurred mortgage debt to decreasing values of home collateral. These concerns cannot be readily dismissed. Debt leverage of all types is often troublesome when one judges the stability of the economy. Should home prices fall, we would have reason to be concerned about mortgage debt; but measures of household financial stress do not, at least to date, appear overly worrisome."

Even with the overall rise in loan-to-value, Greenspan didn't appear to be overly concerned. Although some down payments were borrowed, he noted, "it would take a large, and historically most unusual, fall in home prices to wipe out a significant part of home equity. Many of those who purchased their residence more than a year ago have equity buffers in their homes adequate to withstand any price decline other than a very deep one."[6]

Slice-and-Dice Debt Packages

Declining credit quality, higher loan-to-value ratios, and the prospect of declining housing prices weren't the only troubles brewing. Another factor was the increase in securitization of mortgages. For decades, lenders have been able to benefit from the presence in the second- ary mortgage market of Fannie Mae, which helps ensure that banks and other lenders have enough funds to provide to home buyers, and Freddie Mac, which actively buys loans from lenders. Beyond Fannie and Freddie, the financial market became even more creative when it came to securitizing loans.

Given the demand for yield from investors who were not con- tent with a few percentage points of return, there was ample incentive in the marketplace to create and expand products, such as structured investment vehicles (SIVs) and collateralized debt obligations (CDOs). It all came down to slicing and dicing debt and redistributing risk. Unfortunately, it ended up making the entire system riskier and more prone to a meltdown—and the murky credit default swap market, used to "insured" transactions, added to the fear of the unknown.

In essence, financial institutions were packaging riskier debt that paid a higher rate with other loans, to create products that were bun- dled together and then stripped apart in increasingly complex transac- tions. Here is a hypothetical example that draws upon actual events.

Acme Widget in Indiana is an A-rated company that needed to raise $100 million for an expansion project. Acme approached its bankers about doing a bond offering. With Treasuries at around 5 percent, Acme offered to pay 6 percent. A pension company that was interested in the bonds, however, told the bankers that it needed at least 8 percent to make the investment.

The bankers came up with an innovative solution: They combined Acme's $100 million in bonds paying 6 percent with another $100 million of subprime loans, including home mortgages that were paying around 12 to 13 percent. The combined rate of the debt was 9 percent. The bankers even built in the possibility of some subprime borrowers defaulting.

The package of debt looked like a win for everyone. The pension fund got the rate it wanted on the bond package. Acme was able to finance $100 million at 6 percent, and the people who were given mortgages at 12 to 13 percent would have been ineligible for financing in any other credit environment. Moreover, by combining the low-rated subprime mortgages with the A-rated Acme Widget debt, the pension fund took on a credit investment with an effective rating of B.

The debt didn't stay together as one package, however. After it was bundled together and sold to the pension fund, the debt was later broken apart and the coupons resold. One party agreed to take the subprime tranche, putting up $10 million and borrowing the other $90 million.

Hypothetical? The specifics of this example are, perhaps. But in the very real world, this scenario played out over and over again. As the watch became a warning in the credit market, there were too few players considering what would happen if there weren't just a few defaults but a massive meltdown in the subprime market. As subprime borrowers defaulted, the entire security—not just their portion—would be rendered worthless. In the previous example, even though Acme would continue to make its payments, the value of the entire bond would deteriorate because the higher-yield portion of the debt was not producing anything. Further, whatever investors had been using the income stream from the debt repayment would also become compromised, as that money was no longer available.

One Last Blast to Inflate the Bubble

When does an expansion become a bubble? It's always easier to see this in the rearview mirror. Nonetheless, there were definitely some obvious warning signs as loud and insistent as the emergency broadcast beep when a tornado has been sighted or a severe storm is headed your way. The percentage of subprime mortgage within the overall mortgage portfolios of banks and other lending institutions was on the rise. Some markets saw subprime accounting for nearly half total refinancing.

On the behavioral front, the price of houses became a regular topic of conversation, and not just among people who speculate in real estate. Hearing stories of people who bought a house for "X" and sold it X+Y (or even X *times* Z more), others longed to do the same, even if it meant taking on a second or third mortgage to do so. Also on the behavioral front, Ty Pennington—our unofficial barometer of housing mania—moved from cable to ABC Prime Time. America was officially obsessed with houses.

A Violent Storm: The Bursting of the Bubble

Just as violent weather causes damage beyond the impact of water and wind, the same holds true with an economic storm. The bursting of the credit bubble brought damage far beyond declining home prices. The credit market has tightened, making it harder for individuals and businesses—even those with good credit—to get access to the funds they want or need. Faced with mounting losses, banks have added to their reserves, putting a strain on their own liquidity. Larger institutions initially sought billions in fresh capital, but those infusions were not enough. Banks failed, investment banks sold partial stakes (in the case of Goldman Sachs and Morgan Stanley) or all of the business (Merrill Lynch). Lehman Brothers was allowed to go bankrupt, and its businesses were carved up by Barclays of Britain and Nomura of Japan. Retail banks have also failed: Washington Mutual, the Seattle-based thrift, becoming the largest failure, as it was seized by the FDIC and sold off to JPMorgan Chase. The banking assets of Wachovia were sold while it was an inch from peril to Citigroup in a deal facilitated by the FDIC, which also offered billions in loan-loss guarantees. At the last minute the Wachovia-Citigroup deal was upended when Wells Fargo bid to acquire all of Wachovia.

Homeowners with properties to sell have faced a dearth of buyers and declining prices. Businesses from homebuilders to do-it-yourself and home supply stores have suffered.

Yet all is not lost. There are still cars on the street, businesses are open. Even in the direst of economic times we cannot lose or forget hope. The cyclicality of the economy, in fact, guarantees that once the contraction is spent and a bottom is finally reached, things *will* turn up. It is the dawn that follows the proverbial darkness. There will be an impact on the economy, however; how long and how deep is anyone's guess as of this writing. But we must be cognizant that after a storm of this magnitude, the cleanup will be long and costly.

The Impact on U.S. Economic Growth

In the U.S. economy, the consumer is king. Some two-thirds of our GDP is generated by consumer spending. Thus, when anything interferes with how much consumers spend, or plan on spending, there is an undeniable impact on the economy.

One of the most closely watched economic topics has been the wealth effect. In the 1990s, the wealth effect was studied during the bull market that swelled investment portfolios and the amount of money in 401(k) retirement plans. Because investors felt "wealthier," they became more active consumers. Even during the economic slowdown early in the decade of the 2000s, consumer spending didn't decline much at all. Part of the reason was that the wealth effect was taking root elsewhere: this time in people's homes.

As a recent Congressional Budget Office (CBO) report noted: "At the same time that home prices were rising rapidly during the late 1990s and early 2000s, consumer spending was growing faster than income, as reflected in the falling rate of personal saving. Many observers have concluded that those two facts are linked: that consumers used their growing housing wealth to boost their spending, in effect letting their houses do their saving for them."[7]

Now that housing prices have declined and the credit crisis has led to a liquidity crunch, the impact on consumer spending bears watching as to how much it could impact GDP. This includes reduced consumption as people scale back their spending, but also indirect impact as companies trim back on such things as capital equipment to make consumer goods.

Although there is another school of thought that dismisses or at least diminishes the wealth effect, the impact of the decline in the housing market is undeniable, both in terms of the drop in housing sales as well as the reduction in spending on housing-related goods and services—all of which will show up in slower GDP growth.

But just as we saw a shift in the wealth effect from the stock market to housing, we will see another transition in the future. I strongly believe that some other market will take over and generate gains that will help consumers become, or at least feel, wealthier, and thereby support spending.

That next thing, in my opinion, will be driven by corporate profits and higher equity prices, as opposed to real estate and other assets that are financed. So houses, airports, shopping malls, and office parks may not generate the returns as they did in years past, but the stock market will come back in fashion, if you will.

And that's the bull inside this bear in the wake of the credit bubble implosion.

The Bull Inside the Bear: Lessons from a Housing Bubble

When examining the inflating of the housing bubble, we can cite lending practices, borrowers with lower credit scores, and irrationality in housing prices. But there was another fundamental at work: People viewed their houses as more than just a place to live. Even for people who weren't actively speculating in real estate—such as with a real estate investment trust (REIT) or by buying and selling properties—homes had become "investments." People became acutely aware of how much equity they'd built up, and dreamed of what they could do if they bought bigger, larger, and more expensive, and then *that* property experienced the same kind of exponential growth in value that they'd already witnessed.

During the housing bubble the pattern that emerged was that the first home became an initial "investment" in order to trade up to a second home and then a third one some day. There were plenty of real estate success stories of single people or young couples who bought a condo in the big city, sold it a few years later at a much higher price, and then bought a bigger house in the suburbs. For those who made this transition from house-to-house the timing was fortuitous, but it wasn't to be a permanent phenomenon.

Today, there are people out there who are saddled with two properties: one they couldn't sell and the other they really wanted to buy even though it meant taking on a second mortgage. The reasons for the second property may have been to get out of the city and live in a particular suburb with good schools. Or maybe the first place was fine for one but too small for two (and then three with a baby on the way).

Now that the flipping trend has flopped, we need to uncouple our thinking around housing and investment. A house, loft, or condo is a place to live; not an asset that's "guaranteed" to go up X-percent within a certain time frame.

The upheaval in the housing market may also lead to some rethinking about the timing of a home purchase in one's life. Rather than rush into buying a condo, a young professional may end up renting or even living at home with his or her parents in order to save up for a down payment on a bigger or more valuable property that will fit one's lifestyle for longer than a few years. We may never get back to behaviors of the generation who grew up in or shortly after the Depression, for whom there was no concept of a "starter house." However, house hopping will no longer be the national sport.

Like drinking champagne, the bubbles may be fun while they last, but there can be quite the headache afterwards. In terms of the housing hangover, we expect it to last for a while. If and when prices return to higher levels will depend upon what happens in a time frame measured in multiple years.

Already, however, there have been headlines that suggest that at depressed prices, houses are a "bargain." In the current market and with the right capitalization and credit profile, you may find a well-priced property for a second home, a vacation or retirement property, or because you want to buy a condo for your grandmother. I would repeat the caution here that housing needs to be a decision based upon where one wants to live. This is not about acquiring assets for an investment portfolio. Housing can't be approached the same way as other markets when it comes to investment and speculation. Leave the business of bricks-and-mortar to professional homebuilders, contractors, and developers.

Now if at some time in the future you think that the housing market is looking attractive again and will likely see some increased activity and price appreciation, you can become involved without buying the house down the block to flip or scouting out a vacant lot to build on spec. There are far better and more efficient ways to invest in a sector such as housing.

It can be as simple as buying assets that correlate positively with the housing market; for example, stocks such as Home Depot. Or you might want to buy a housing ETF: an exchange-traded fund that is bought and sold like a stock and replicates a specific index or sector. You could also invest in certain REITS whose portfolios correlate with your investment objective.

As for your own home sweet home, appreciate it as a place to live, whether it's a lot in the city or a house in the distant ex-burbs. This is your home, your castle—not your ATM machine.

Chapter 6

The Fed as FEMA

Much will be written about the styles of three very different chairmen of the Federal Reserve. Paul Volcker fought inflation. Alan Greenspan instituted the equity markets as the feel-good benchmark and rescued stocks at every dip. If success is measured by the compounding return on stocks, Greenspan did a very good job. And now it is Ben Bernanke's turn at the helm. As Bernanke fights to contain the damage from the housing and credit bubbles, he has had to use other tools than those employed by his predecessors. Volcker hiked rates and saved the day. Greenspan lowered them to save the day. Bernanke had to resort to unprecedented, even extreme measures, to intervene in the capital markets.

There have been some times when the Fed needed to intervene; for example when the Volcker Fed battled double-digit inflation. But I do have to wonder if the level of intervention undertaken by the Fed in every instance has been necessary. Perhaps the markets would have corrected themselves without the Fed chairmen intervening on certain occasions. More recently, the bailout engineered by Treasury Secretary Henry Paulson in conjunction with Bernanke stuck me at first as an unacceptable level of intervention, but ultimately appeared necessary.

Looking at the Greenspan years in particular, I have to question whether the amount of liquidity pumped into the marketplace was needed. Yes, the pain might have lasted longer and the cycles probably would have been shorter and more volatile. Nonetheless, the cycles still would have occurred. More importantly, some of the problems may not have surfaced later on: specifically, the flush of liquidity may not have resulted in "easy money" in the credit markets.

This leads to some "Monday morning quarterbacking" on the Fed's actions as we review the actions taken. I don't want to appear to be blaming the Fed for all an financial problems. Looking back, however, we must ask: Did Long-Term Capital Management (LTCM), the hedge fund that experienced the infamous meltdown in the late 1990s, really need to be saved? Did we need all the extra liquidity that was pumped into the system before Y2K? And what about Bear Stearns? Did the Fed really have to play matchmaker to orchestrate the acquisition of Bear Stearns by JPMorgan Chase? Since Lehman Brothers was allowed to go bankrupt (supposedly because it did not act swiftly enough to address its problems) why were extraordinary measures taken for Bear Stearns?

The broader question is, does the Fed have to play nursemaid to the economy at every turn? Children without a bedtime do eventually fall asleep. And so it may very well be with the economy and the financial system if the troubles are allowed to work their way out. If Wall Street, banks, and the financial system in general know that whatever risks they take on, the Fed will always be there to get them out of a jam, what message does that send? Risk management needs to begin "at home" with those that are creating the risks in the first place. While the marketplace loves to securitize and hedge its way toward a "risk-free" investment vehicle, time and again we've seen that such an animal doesn't exist. Just as LTCM's supposedly perfectly hedged portfolio went haywire when Russia defaulted on its domestic debt, risks have a way of creeping into the system. And when they do, the Fed is there, ready with the rescue.

The Fed to the Rescue

As the aftermath of the credit crisis unfolded, the federal government has taken strong actions to intervene both in the markets and in the financial services industry. This level of intervention brings to mind the role of the Federal Emergency Management Administration (FEMA) after a natural disaster such as a hurricane. While FEMA is expected to mobilize to mitigate the impact on people, businesses, and infrastructure—reducing the level of disruption, discomfort, and suffering—we don't expect the same kind of direct involvement when it comes to the Federal Reserve.

In this chapter, we will discuss the unprecedented role of "Fed as FEMA" as the Federal Reserve, led by Chairman Bernanke, increased its authorities to intervene and manage the impact on the markets and the financial services industry after the bursting of the credit bubble. As history has shown us, whenever a governmental entity expands its powers, rarely are they rescinded. With the Federal Reserve, the broader scope of influence will continue into the future, although certain powers may not be exercised on a regular basis.

For you, as an investor, the expanded role of the Fed creates opportunities. The bolder the action taken by the Fed, the more liquidity and incentives will be pumped into the system one way or another. This liquidity, along with other incentives like tax breaks and federal support, will flow not only into sectors that have been damaged, but also those that are relatively strong. Knowing the differences will help you to find investment opportunities in the future—particularly those opportunities when the proverbial wind is at your back—and to take advantage of the bull inside the bear.

A Short History of the Fed

The United States has not always had a central bank. In fact, at the founding of this country the idea of a strong centralized bank was opposed. Treasury Secretary Alexander Hamilton urged the establishment of the First Bank of the United States in 1791, which was then the largest corporation in the country. But when its 20-year charter expired,

Congress did not renew it because of opposition to a large and powerful central bank. The Second Bank of the United States was chartered in 1816, but it did not survive renewal when its charter expired in 1836.

By 1912, a proposal known as Glass-Willis was developed, which would become the Federal Reserve Act, and in 1913 the Federal Reserve System was established as a "decentralized central bank." By the 1920s, the Fed had begun exercising the power of open market operations to influence the availability of credit in the banking system. The open market operation soon became a powerful tool for monetary policy.

After the Great Depression, Congress passed several banking regulations, among them the Banking Act of 1933—also known as Glass-Steagall—which called for the separation of commercial and investment banking. Among other provisions, the Banking Act of 1933 placed open market operations under the Fed and required bank holding companies to be examined by the Fed. The Banking Act of 1935 made additional changes in the Fed's structure, including the Federal Open Market Commission (FOMC), which was created as a separate legal entity.

As policies and regulations surrounding the Fed and banking evolved and were adopted, among the newer developments was the Humphrey-Hawkins Act, which requires the Fed chairman to report to Congress twice a year on monetary policy goals and objectives. Humphrey-Hawkins testimony is closely watched not only for the Fed's analysis of the state of the economy, but also for what actions the Fed might take—whether to combat inflation, stimulate the economy, or cool down an overheating economy.

The Fed Steps In

Although the Fed has faced its share of critics over the years—including President John F. Kennedy, who supposedly wanted to put the Fed out of business—it remains the key watchdog of the economy and wields incredible power to set monetary policy. One of the strongest examples of the Fed's iron fist of control was during the 1980s when the United States faced skyrocketing inflation. Producer prices and consumer prices were on the rise and the Federal deficit more than doubled. It became Paul Volcker's job, after being sworn in as Fed chairman in August 1979, to bring double-digit inflation under control. As stated previously, Volcker administered the strong medicine to whip inflation, even though it did yank the United States into a double-dip recession.

Of all the interventions undertaken by the Fed, I believe Volcker's actions to counter the insidious effects of inflation on the economy were the most warranted—until now. Without strong action by the Volcker Fed, the U.S. economy could have suffered even more damage due to longer term double-digit inflation.

Also, as stated previously, the bailout of the banking system after the savings and loan (S&L) crisis of the 1980s and 1990s was masterful. It brought together a variety of federal entities, including the FDIC, the Office of Thrift Supervision, and the newly formed Resolution Trust Corporation. The Fed's role was very instrumental in how the banks that were taken over in the wake of the S&L crisis would be treated. As the S&L crisis was sorted out, the Fed was largely in the background, although completely appropriate given the impact on banking.

There have been other points in time, however, when the Fed took bold action in response to a crisis or perceived crisis, which in retrospect seems to have been an overreaction. As we've seen more recently, with the Bernanke-led Fed's actions after the credit crisis and to help broker the Bear Stearns-JPMorgan deal, the Fed is making bolder moves with broader implications. To be clear, the Fed has not taken on powers that are completely outside its jurisdiction. Rather, the Fed's actions are an expansion from its traditional roles and responsibilities. As long as the Fed can connect the dots back to the health of the economy and to provide full employment without creating inflation, it can make the case that it is fulfilling its mandate.

Greenspan and the Stock Market

A question mark hangs over the Federal Reserve's actions where the stock market is concerned. As we saw immediately following the 1987 crash (which, as we described in Chapter 2, was really a "blip" due to a technical glitch) the Fed provided additional liquidity by reversing a previous rate hike and reducing rates even further. Greenspan also broadcast in a one-sentence statement the assurance that whatever liquidity the marketplace needed the Fed would provide.

Greenspan connected the dots between intervening to help the stock market with its primary responsibility of monitoring the health and the stability of the economy. While the economy and the stock market are separate, under Greenspan there was a blurring of the two.

In addition to using traditional tools of interest rate movement to affect liquidity, the Fed took other actions as well in October 1987. There were sophisticated transactions in the options market orchestrated by the Fed to help ensure that the exchanges would be able to meet their financial obligations.

The Fed also became directly involved with the operations of First Options of Chicago, Inc., a large trading and clearing institution for the Chicago Board Options Exchange (CBOE), which was owned by Continental Illinois. The problems for the clearing firm began after some of its customers suffered significant losses and were unable to meet margin calls. First Options then faced its own margin calls, and needed financing. "The Federal Reserve acted to enable Continental Illinois, parent company of First Options, to inject funds into the subsidiary. Without these funds, First Options would likely not have been able to open which reportedly would have caused serious problems for the operations of the options exchange," a Federal Reserve analysis of actions taken after the 1987 crash stated.[1]

When the "crash" of 1987 occurred, the Fed took action because of what it saw as the potential impact on banks, brokerages, and clearing firms, and also because of the perception of bigger risk to the economy as a whole. The Fed's actions to support the clearing mechanisms of the exchanges was very similar to how it would have encouraged the takeover of a bank that was failing.

The dotted line of Federal Reserve responsibility where clearing firms such as First Options were concerned led to the fact that many of these operations had strong relationships with banks or were owned by them. Regardless of the dotted line or the perception of risk to the financial system as a whole, this was a significant example of the Fed to the rescue.

More important, the Fed's intervention on behalf of First Options appears to eerily presage what it did when Bear Stearns faced bankruptcy after experiencing a liquidity run. As we'll discuss later in this chapter, with the Bear Stearns intervention, the Fed leapfrogged into a whole new area of involvement. While it is widely believed that there was a "greater good" theory going on supporting rescuing or arranging a rescue package for these financial institutions, my guess is that we will never know for sure. It is true that confidence in the banking system is essential for the economy to work, but the "too big to fail" theory provides incentives for the wrong behavior. It privatizes profits while socializing losses. I have strong views of right or wrong on this topic and others, but will save my rants for now. Here, I want to focus on facts and theories to inform the reader on the history and mechanisms that shape the economy and markets. This will enable you to find the bull inside the bear.

Greenspan and Liquidity

Throughout much of the 1990s, Greenspan's finger remained on the liquidity button, which was possible given the low-inflation environment at the time. Throughout the 1990s, the Fed used monetary policy on a number of occasions—including the credit crunch of the early 1990s and the Russian default on government bonds.

This short history, however, doesn't do justice to the scope of actions taken during the decade of the 1990s: among them the intervention following the failure of LTCM, an event which gets unfairly cited more than it deserves as a pivotal or catastrophic event. But far be it from me to deviate from the pattern. The very long story made short, LTCM used high leverage and invested in exotic and often illiquid markets in hopes of producing returns for investors. It was all "perfectly hedged" until Russia defaulted on its domestic debt, and the LTCM portfolio came tumbling down.

According to Greenspan's testimony before Congress in October 1998, the Federal Reserve Bank of New York (which 10 years later would play a key role in the Bear Stearns bailout) became concerned about the impact of LTCM's portfolio in a forced liquidation, which "would not only have a significant distorting impact on market prices but also in the process could produce large losses, or worse, for a number of creditors and counterparties, and for other market participants who were not directly involved with LTCM."

Instead of holding a "disorderly fire sale," the Federal Reserve Bank of New York sought alternatives to bankruptcy. (If this is sounding oddly familiar, remember this is LTCM we're talking about, not Bear Stearns—yet.) On September 23, 1998, private sector parties agreed to provide a capital infusion of about $3.5 billion. Control of the firm was given to a committee chosen by new investors.[2]

As the Fed stepped in and arranged for other hedge funds and investment banks to buy LTCM assets, my guess is that there could have been some swap arrangements and financing put in place to safeguard the consortium of private parties that found itself with worthless assets. And those safeguards, if they indeed existed, would have been linked right back to the Fed. While it's conjecture on my part, it certainly seems plausible.

In his October 1998 testimony, Greenspan painted the Fed's actions as necessary to safeguard the financial system, including banks as he carefully connected the dots back to the central bank's main area of responsibility, namely the health of the economy. While I suppose one could argue that the Fed acted with alacrity to step in to avoid the LTCM asset fire sale, I have to question if the meltdown of one hedge fund—which was worth some $2 or $3 billion—really would have put the financial markets on the brink.

The LTCM issue was overleverage of assets that still had value. The problem was that value had gone well below where it started as collateral. But it didn't all just "disappear." It's like a $1 million property with an $800,000 mortgage. The property becomes devalued and is now worth $700,000. It still has an $800,000 mortgage, which is more debt than what the property is worth. But the asset is still worth something. While the decline in asset value is a hardship and, yes, a fire sale can further pressure the values of other assets in the marketplace, that's part of the risk.

If we look to the Federal Reserve to bail out the marketplace because someone has taken on too much risk, then that completely negates the responsibility of the parties involved to do their own risk management and keep their own house in order. It's like the parent who sends a kid off to college with a checking account and a stiff warning about managing money, not spending foolishly, and never being overdrawn—then at the first sign of trouble pumps another thousand into the account. Do you think that will teach Johnny or Jill to be more prudent?

Liquidity Flows and Flows

When the dust settled around LTCM, the Fed continued an accommodative stance to bolster the economy through the end of the decade—
and of the century. The infamous Y2K had everyone pondering and
pontificating about the effect of the "century change date" on computers everywhere. Would the rollover from 12/31/99 to 01/01/00 cause
havoc and mass hysteria? Would systems, from banking to aviation, be
in danger of crashing?

While computer firms, programmers, and installers made a tidy fortune in Y2K preparedness, the Fed stepped in with, what else, liquidity.
As far as the Fed was concerned, the risks were too big to take a wait-
and-see attitude. In a speech before a summit on year 2000 preparedness, Greenspan painted a picture of what *could* conceivably happen if
Y2K glitches became widespread.

"Although the banking system and ATM providers are about as
prepared for Y2K as they can be, we cannot realistically expect perfec-
tion over the New Year's holiday any more than at similar periods in
years past. Moreover, while systems may fail as they have in the past,
these failures never have resulted in broader and persistent—that is,
systemic—breakdowns in our economy. Notwithstanding, it is at least
conceivable that, as a consequence of our current dependence on computers, some Y2K-related failures could have noticeable effects on the
economy," Greenspan stated.[3]

However, thanks to $50 billion of private sector expenditures,
enough of the infrastructure had been made Y2K-compliant to avert a
system breakdown, Greenspan added. Nonetheless, the Fed stood ready
with liquidity—just in case—through a Century Date Change Special
Liquidity Facility of the discount window and contingency actions of
the FOMC "to help ensure an ample supply of liquidity and relieve
funding pressure."

Then came September 11, 2001, and the Fed responded with
liquidity. To a lesser extent, the fallout from the corporate malfeasance
scandals of the early 2000s was also managed, in some form or other,
by the Fed's accommodative stance.

The sum total of the Fed's action was to have an economy that was
dripping with liquidity. And where did it go? As previously stated, the

liquidity of the 1990s found its way into the stock market, helping to create a bubble—especially in tech stocks. In the 2000s, liquidity that was the remedy for the bursting of the tech bubble found its way into housing, which experienced a dramatic price escalation as the credit bubble inflated.

These cause-and-effect circumstances make me question the wisdom of having the Fed intervene every time there is a perceived threat, whether to the economy or the market. I understand and support the role of the Fed to control inflation (as Volcker did in the 1980s) or to stimulate the economy (as has occurred many times) but providing extra liquidity to keep the stock market from selling off is a stretch to me. The Fed's role is to guide the economy and achieve full employment. But if there are developments that could hurt stock prices, then people are going to sell. Stock prices will decline, perhaps even dramatically, and then at some point buyers will step in and equilibrium will be restored. Does the Fed need to intervene and provide liquidity in that scenario? The Fed's job is not to prop up the stock market. Although there are plenty of dotted lines that connect the economy and the stock market, I believe the Fed needs to mind the boundaries for the long-term health of the economy.

I don't want to blame the Fed for every liquidity-related problem that the economy has been having recently. Not even Greenspan himself could have foreseen the velocity at which liquidity would travel through the banking system. The innovative structured products and so-called risk management programs encouraged lending at an unrealistic pace—including providing loans to borrowers with credit ratings that would not be able sustain the debt burden. However, by trying to solve all the little problems the smoldering big problem grows, eventually taking everything down with it.

Bailing out Bear Stearns

When the credit bubble burst, damage splattered across the economic landscape: foreclosures, a slowing of the real estate market, tighter credit for businesses and consumers, and some real problems for financial institutions. Banks suddenly faced credit losses and mortgage defaults. More damaging were the speculative positions taken in mortgage-related derivatives—including collateralized debt obligations (CDOs) and structured investment vehicles (SIVs)—that created billions in losses for hedge funds and investment banks.

At one investment bank in particular, Bear Stearns, the implosion of the subprime credit market caused steep losses at two of its hedge funds to the tune of $1.6 billion in investor money. The losses for Bear Stearns didn't stop there. Concerns about its liquidity—which apparently were unfounded—caused investors to pull money from their accounts and prompted counterparties to discontinue trading with Bear Stearns. By Thursday March 13, 2008, the problem was so severe, Bear Stearns appealed for help and the Federal Reserve and the Treasury Department stepped in with a rescue plan. On Friday March 14, 2008, JPMorgan Chase had agreed to act as a go-between in a pass-through financing deal that would allow the Fed to provide liquidity to Bear Stearns via JPMorgan. As a commercial bank, JPMorgan was under the Fed's purview and had access to the discount window. By the weekend, it was decided that Bear Stearns would have to declare bankruptcy on the morning of Monday March 17 unless a party could be found to buy the ailing investment bank. That party was JPMorgan, in what was at first a $2-a-share deal (later raised to $10-a-share to placate angry Bear Stearns shareholders). The transaction was brokered by the Treasury and the Fed, which used special emergency authorities to facilitate the acquisition. This special help amounted to $29 billion in financing to JPMorgan to offset the impact of illiquid assets on the Bear Stearns' books.

In testimony before Congress in July 2008, Fed Chairman Bernanke used dire terms as he described Bear Stearns being "pushed to the brink of failure," which would "pose a serious threat to overall financial stability and would most likely have significant adverse implications for the U.S. economy."[4]

His statement can be seen countering criticism that the Fed had gone too far over the line in its intervention to save an investment bank, which is outside its authority. By invoking the perceived threat to the economy and the financial system, however, Bernanke put the Bear Stearns deal under the Fed's authority and justified use of several "emergency authorities" that expanded the power and scope of the central bank.

Under its emergency authorities, the Fed established two new facilities to provide liquidity to primary dealers. In testimony, Bernanke said the goal was to stabilize financial conditions and increase the availability of credit made available to banks through the Term Auction Facility. The FOMC also expanded currency swap arrangements with the European Central Bank and the Swiss National Bank to increase dollar lending by those institutions to banks in their jurisdictions.

Whether or not the Fed should have intervened to save Bear Stearns from bankruptcy can and will be argued for some time. If, indeed, the aversion of a Bear Stearns bankruptcy stabilized the market and avoided damaging shocks to the economy, then the Fed did not overstep its bounds. But it should be noted that, in the months immediately following the JPMorgan acquisition of Bear Stearns, the stock market and the economy as a whole have worsened. The stock market is lower and more jobs have been lost. Of course, someone could argue that, without the Bear Stearns deal, things would have been worse. But if we're going to connect the dots from Fed action back to the economy, we need to look at the picture realistically.

Bernanke told Congress that the "steps to address liquidity pressures coupled with monetary easing seem to have been helpful in mitigating some market strains." However, several issues remained, including the financial health of two government-sponsored enterprises, Fannie Mae and Freddie Mac, which facilitate homeowner borrowing. Also of concern was high inflation, concern over a slow-growing economy, and fears of a recession. Noting that "healthy economic growth depends on well-functioning financial markets," Bernanke pledged to help "the financial markets to return to more normal functioning."[5]

As he takes on that task, Bernanke cannot follow in Greenspan's steps to keep lowering rates to help boost the economy. Rates are already low and inflation will soon become a major concern. Therefore, we can expect more creativity out of the Bernanke Fed to manage the economy and provide liquidity.

As he takes on that task, Bernanke cannot follow in Greenspan's steps to keep lowering rates to help boost the economy. Rates are already low and inflation will become a major concern in the not-so-distant future. Therefore, we can expect more creativity out of the Bernanke Fed to manage the economy and provide liquidity.

With a changing of the guard under the Obama administration we are seeing new players take on monumental challenges posed by the economy and an ailing Wall Street. Timothy Geithner, who has served under three presidents, most recently as president and CEO of the Federal Reserve Bank of New York, has taken over as Treasury Secretary. Controversial, but respected, Larry Summers, is the new director of the National Economic Council. Summers served previously as Secretary of the Treasury (1999-2001), president of Harvard University (2001-2006), and as a top economist at the World Bank. Mary Schapiro, the new chair of the Securities and Exchange Commission (SEC), has previously served as CEO of the Financial Industry Regulatory Authority and as chair of the federal Commodity Futures Trading Commission (CFTC).

Looking at their backgrounds, it's apparent that these new players will likely have an agenda to put procedures in place that go beyond the occasional bank failure or hedge-fund blowup. We could very well see a massive "defense system" to prevent global financial meltdowns in the future. That would require greater coordination among central bankers, Congress, the President, business leaders, and international markets. Another potential outcome could be the merging, or at least far greater coordination, between the SEC and the CFTC, with an eye toward more extensive oversight of the financial industry.

If we've learned one thing from the current crisis, it is how pervasive and integrated problems really are; for example, a credit crisis that hit banks and Wall Street first coming home in the auto industry, and Congressional banking committees involved in talks about a possible bailout for Detroit. Moving forward, tackling problems in the economy and on Wall Street will require—ideally—coordination from the best and brightest. While poor at self-regulating, Wall Street will undoubtedly press for regulations that will keep the implosions at bay while not curtailing innovation and, of course, profitability. It's a tall order, and we can only wait to see what solutions and programs emerge in time.

The Hidden Cost of Fed as FEMA

When the Fed acts like FEMA, sometimes it helps to stabilize a market and create an orderly transition, thus guiding the capitalism train back on track. A perfect example is the bailout of the savings and loans (S&L) in the early 1990s. Such actions, however, are not without cost. The hidden costs of the S&L intervention were artificially high interest rates and restrictive lending policies. In this case, however, the clean-up worked and the cost appeared well worth it.

More importantly, how do these bailouts differ from what we saw in S&Ls in the early 1990s? This question holds the key, in my view. The S&L bailout was for an entire industry, not an individual entity. If intervention supports one firm over another it not only sets a bad example, but it doesn't solve the problem. Hence, after the rescue package for Bear Stearns, the market turned for a few weeks with the rallying cry, "Fed to the Rescue"—or maybe "Fed as FEMA!" But when the next hurricane-like problem hit the market, it was clear that nothing was solved.

Rather than committing so many resources to get one victim out of danger, it would be better to expand preparation. To use the natural disaster analogy, there would be a far better outcome if energy and resources were directed to setting up guidelines and rules to prepare for potential hurricanes: sell water, generators, and lumber to secure and protect structures; map out evacuation routes. Thus preparation would result in a better solution for everyone. But using the resources to rescue one victim is counterproductive.

The lesson for the financial markets is if instead of supporting $29 billion in loan guarantees for JPMorgan, without which it would have not stepped up to buy Bear Stearns, what if the Fed had instead used that money to set up some liquidity financial vehicle? This measure would have added liquidity to the system, but with a penalty for use. The result would be a better mechanism to deal with the "too big to fail" institutions.

I remember being a currency dealer at Bank of America when Drexel collapsed. No one would accept Drexel's name in a foreign exchange trade, which created a domino effect and eventually Drexel went bankrupt. Knowing the only risk was exchange rate movement, I considered it important to honor their trades as not doing so would create a bigger issue for me and the system at large. Although Drexel did die that day, its trades were honored and the system didn't collapse. Maybe a lesson to be learned is that you can save your children from a burning house without having to save the house. You will be able to find another home.

The Fed's responsibility is to make sure rules and guidelines are in place to be able to monitor activities so failure is not an option. They might need to blow the whistle at times; call a time out to regroup and then get the game going again. But it's not the Fed's place to actually get in the game and hog the ball. That will mean that in times of crisis, institutions fail; equity gets wiped out; debt is defaulted on; and the normal bankruptcy laws apply—albeit with special laws regarding financial institutions to deal with the specific intricacies of this business. Then, transactions that support other transactions should be guaranteed by the Fed either directly or as a guarantor of another institution that will facilitate the transaction.

This is one person's opinion, of course, and the Fed will do what it will do. But at some point we have to ask ourselves why, when, and how should the Fed act as FEMA—and when is intervention too much meddling in what should be free markets.

The Bull Inside the Bear: The Fed, Intervention, and You

As the spillover from the credit crisis continues to be mopped up, it's likely that we'll see even more "emergency actions" from the Fed in conjunction with the Treasury Department. Such actions expand the Fed's muscle beyond its more historic limits.

Once the Fed exercises emergency authorities, it's not likely that it will suddenly rescind them. Even though it may not use these powers on a regular basis, once they've been used, they will be part of the Fed toolbox. And as we've seen, emergency authorities can be expanded in the future should conditions warrant it.

The precedence of Fed intervention provides some real opportunities for investors. As we've seen, the Fed's response to just about any situation—real, perceived, or potential—is to provide liquidity. Sometimes it's after the fact, such as when the tech bubble burst, and sometimes it's a preemptive strike, such as Y2K. Liquidity flowing into the economy will find its way to many places. In the 1990s, the liquidity meant to stimulate the economy ended up in the stock market, and the rise of new technology created a bubble in tech stocks. In the late 1990s and through the 2000s, liquidity that was meant to help stabilize the stock market flowed into another area, contributing to a credit bubble and a run-up in housing prices and buying activity.

Now the question is where will the liquidity meant to counter the credit crisis end up? Yes, some of it will help to mitigate damage from the credit crisis. But it will also flow into other, healthier sectors. As I've discussed earlier in this book and as I'll elaborate further in Part III, the next sector to benefit from liquidity will be equities.

As an investor, keeping an eye on Fed policies will give you insight into how much liquidity is flowing and where it might end up next. Past examples show that the beneficiaries of Fed actions include healthy sectors that will use the liquidity to fuel an expansion. After all, when the Fed pumped more money into the economy after the tech bubble burst, housing wasn't in trouble. But the flow of liquidity sure helped to elevate that sector, to the extent that an expansion (bull market) became a bubble.

The bull inside the bear here is that the Federal Reserve to the rescue is usually overkill. It will stimulate parts of the economy that are not damaged and create expansion opportunities. Going back to the FEMA example, it's analogous to hurricane relief in Florida stimulating the economy in California. Why? Because as businesses in Florida rebuilt they bought computers from California.

The Rothschilds supposedly advised that the time to buy was when "there was blood running in the streets." While some may make a fortune by picking up underpriced, valuable assets when the world is awash in red ink, there is a better way. That is to avoid the sector in trouble and to look elsewhere for healthy parts of the economy or another market that seems ready for an expansion. And when the liquidity starts flowing that way, look for the bull inside the bear.

Chapter 7

Your Next Opportunity

The credit crisis. The bursting of the housing bubble. A period of deflation and the looming return of inflation. An economy that has slipped into recession. Because of the confluence of these factors, many investors are concerned that this time is like no other. Inflation makes them think it's the 1970s and we'll soon see double-digit interest rates. They see the housing bubble and think tech stocks, and then suddenly it's 1999 to 2000. Fears of a recession make them wonder if it's going to be a long haul like the double-dip of the 1980s. Is the $700 billion credit-crisis bailout plan going to help or hurt, as the United States faces a situation that some people compare to the Great Depression of the 1930s? At the very least investors are confused and at most scared to death.

If you ask me, I'd say it's clearly *not* like the Great Depression. A depression is not only a prolonged recession but it's characterized by exponentially higher unemployment (as high as 20 percent), as much as a 10 percent decline in GDP lasting four or more quarters. It's essentially an economy that's come to a standstill. Nor is it the late 1970s, early 1980s. If anything, it is similar to the early 1990s. While the economy is slowing down, and unemployment is increasing, the bigger issue is the credit crisis—and more specifically the breakdown of the financial system. The tenuous condition of the overall financial sector—including some of the largest banks, quasi-government agencies, and large investment houses whose existence are part and parcel to the daily functioning of the system—is clearly more the immediate concern. Our economy survives recessions and can combat inflation, but a meltdown of the system that supports the economy is a different story. Inflation is not the front page story, although it will be in the future. First we have to survive the credit crisis, and then we must prepare for a change in long-term economic fundamentals like inflation.

If we can take anything from history, the credit and housing debacle most closely resembles the savings and loan (S&L) crisis, especially the way the Fed has taken strong measures to keep things in control. New government powers and agencies were created to deal with the S&L mess, major banks thought to be too big to fail were on watch lists with federal regulators, and contingency plans were being drafted to support the system should the unthinkable happen. Today, there are real concerns of additional bank failures and defaults on securities that have found their way into the portfolios of investment banks, pension funds, and government agencies. The mere whisper of a default on these securities or by agencies like Freddie and Fannies that guarantee these securities has sent shock waves down Wall Street and Main Street.

Ultimately the fears came to fruition and defaults, bankruptcies, and insolvencies occurred. In the midst of all them, Washington Mutual, a $307 billion Seattle-based thrift, became the largest bank failure in history. The Federal Insurance Deposit Corporation (FDIC) seized Washington Mutual and then sold off most of it to JPMorgan Chase in a $1.9 billion deal. The money went into FDIC coffers, as it should, while investors—including those that had very recently put up $7 billion in private equity—were out in the cold. In the midst of the government orchestrating gigantic bailouts, the WaMu deal stood out as the way things are supposed to work. A bank fails, the federal government takes it over, and the assets and certain liabilities are sold. There was no taxpayer money involved, just a neat and tidy deal that kept the bank running and—most important—preserved the insured *and* noninsured deposits.

This point is too often lost on consumers, who in the midst of the credit crisis have opted for putting their cash under the mattress instead of leaving it in the bank. Even if a bank fails, insured deposits (raised in 2008 to $250,000 on a regular checking or savings account), are backed by the FDIC, and even uninsured deposits are rarely in danger. The chance of losing one's money if a bank fails is zero for insured deposits, and only 1 to 2 percent likely for uninsured deposits. The WaMu failure showed us just exactly how that was supposed to work.

All of these events, however, have created even more uncertainty about the future of the economy and the financial system. While as dire as this all sounds, this is setting up the next opportunity on the horizon, which I'll tell you about shortly.

Many investors, today, however, can't see the proverbial forest for the trees. They can't consider the opportunities because all they can focus on is what used to be: housing prices that were all but guaranteed to go up; easy credit for mortgages and refinancing; and the ability to pull out equity to close a budget gap or to pay for "extras" from an addition on the house to a vacation. The housing market isn't what it once was, and perhaps won't be again for at least a decade. Home sales in 2008 and housing prices both remain well below what they were a year earlier, which was already a slower marketplace. Add to that the Fed's warnings about inflation, particularly in energy and food prices, and concerns about an economic slowdown that could slip into recession—or maybe already has (at least in the minds of many consumers).

Admittedly these kinds of conditions are more likely to lead to someone wanting to head for cover, rather than venture out into the storm looking for a rainbow. But that's precisely what forward-looking investors should be doing. Now, I'm not suggesting that anyone dive into the market head first. Nor am I saying "wait for my signal" because of some strategy to pinpoint the absolutely top of one market or the precise bottom of another. I'm saying that—as I've stated repeatedly throughout this book—there *is* a bull inside the bear.

The policies to bail out and support ailing financial institutions will create a tremendous opportunity and the potential for a significant expansion in the asset class that held up best and will have profits to show. That opportunity will be found in the good ol' American corporation and their stocks. In fact, we could even have a repeat of the 1990s bull market. When? Most likely beginning later in 2009, with an expected expansion to be under way in earnest in 2010 and beyond. Why? Because corporate profits will be made again, bonuses will be paid, and investors who were burned by borrowing and buying real estate will find it easier and more efficient to invest in stocks. Plus, consumer spending that completely dried up in late 2008, will gradually resume. And with the explosion in ETFs, investors can target specific investment objectives with a single equity security.

As corporate profits grow, stocks will attract a liquidity flowing from the staggering levels of cash on the side lines. What we've seen in late 2008 in particular is investors who were eager to avoid the declines in stocks park their money in short-term Treasuries. These Treasuries, however, are yielding levels below inflation. But the safety of losing 1 percent rather than 20 percent is appealing, at least in the short run. Once the storm passes and visibility becomes clear, cash will not accept a negative return and will flow out of Treasuries (so be careful of the upcoming bond market decline) and into equities. The sectors leading the way will be identified by employment growth.

Take Heart—Or at Least Take Heed

Whenever there is a contraction in the market or a recession ratchets back the economy, there is usually a catalyst. In 1999 and 2000, the first shoe to drop was the bursting of the tech stock bubble. It wasn't just a few high-flying dot-com shares that had the air taken out of them— the broader market also suffered. First it spread from tech to Nasdaq. And then some smarty-pants pundits said, "This is going to bleed into the rest of the economy." Sure enough, before too long and with some other downward pressures, including Enron and Worldcom troubles, we were in a contraction.

Even though the stock market contracted and the economy slowed, it wasn't all bearish at the time. There were relative bright spots. Some sectors were not suffering as much as others and some even appreciated. For example, as Figure 7.1 shows, small cap stocks made gains in

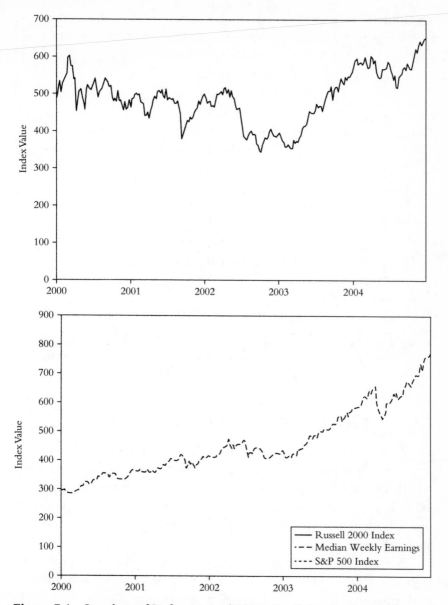

Figure 7.1 Snapshots of Performance of REITs, Small Cap Stocks, and the S&L 500 for 2000–2008

SOURCE: Standard & Poor's (S&P): Central Inquiry Office; Moody's Economy.com. Reproduced with permission of Yahoo! Inc. ® 2008 by Yahoo! Inc. YAHOO! and the YAHOO! logo are trademarks of Yahoo! Inc.

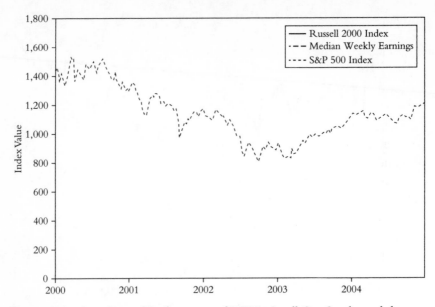

Figure 7.1   Snapshots of Performance of REITs, Small Cap Stocks, and the S&L 500 for 2000–2008. (Continued)
SOURCE: Standard & Poor's (S&P): Central Inquiry Office; Moody's Economy.com. Reproduced with permission of Yahoo! Inc. ® 2008 by Yahoo! Inc. YAHOO! and the YAHOO! logo are trademarks of Yahoo! Inc.

the early 2000s and real estate investment trusts (REITS) performed fairly well.

Now we're in a similar situation. The catalyst is the bursting of the housing market bubble and the credit crunch. We saw the damage first in stocks that were on the front line: mortgage companies and other lenders that were facing hefty subprime losses. Quickly the damage spread, and people because fearful of which companies could be involved next.

The stock market held up initially, but declined heavily in the second half of the 2008, setting it up for the worst year for stock market performance ever. Even so, I don't buy the notion that financial stocks are going to sink the whole economy. That's why I advise investors to take heart; there is a bull inside the bear. And while you may have to be patient and a little discerning, the time is coming for the start of what should be a prolonged expansion in equities, which will be addressed in detail later in this chapter.

Understanding Current Events

To understand our current economic conditions, and therefore the opportunities being presented, we must look at the present in the context of the past. This helps to keep things in perspective that the sky really isn't falling and financial Armageddon isn't upon us.

First, the credit crisis. It's easy to get nervous with all the statistics that are being discussed these days: home foreclosures are up, home sales and prices are down, credit is tighter, big banks are warning that their profits will be hurt by more charge-offs for bad loans, large banks and investment banks are failing and going bankrupt. The news makes it sound like the credit crisis is getting worse. However, it's still the same credit crisis. What we're seeing is the same mess—it's just bigger than we realized.

To use a simple analogy, imagine that you spill grape juice in the refrigerator. You clear off the shelf and mop up the mess. There, it's finished, you say to yourself. But the next time you go into the refrigerator you find grape juice on another shelf and along the back wall as well. Has there been a second spill? No, it's just that the first one spread farther than you thought. Get it? The subprime loan debacle is over as far as the cause is concerned, but the effects are still being felt. Lending policies are tighter and banks are getting their financial houses in order. Insolvent banks are being taken over, and those that need help are being shored up. In fact, I am not surprised to see a revival of the old Resolution Trust Corporation (RTC), which in the 1990s was formed to take over and dispose of assets of bankrupt S&Ls. Whether they end up calling it the RTC or something else, the function will be the same: to take over, manage, and dispose of assets from this credit crisis.

As I've stated previously, I believe the S&L crisis of the 1990s was the worst threat we have faced since the Crash of 1929 and the Great Depression. The federal government's ability to deal with that disaster swiftly and with a minimum of disruption gives me great hope that the same thing can and will happen again as the mess from the credit crisis is mopped up—although it has been pretty ugly in the midst of it. In fact, I believe that we'll see a return to the S&L crisis-era policies: borrow at, say 4 percent, and loan to the federal government at 8 percent, or some similar spread that enables the banking system to get healthy

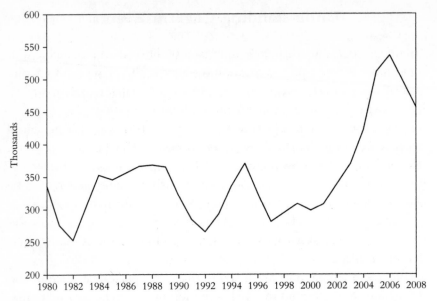

Figure 7.2   U.S. Single Family Houses for Sale 1980–2008
SOURCE: U.S. Census Bureau.

again. In time, lending policies will loosen, and we'll eventually see the credit and housing markets stabilize and perhaps even grow. Growth in the housing market, however, won't happen any time soon. So if you're looking for an expansion there, you'll be disappointed. Much needs to be worked out before we get to a stable housing market with valuations in line with the fundamentals of the property, not the dynamics of the credit market (see Figure 7.2).

Second, the economy. As I stated, the current conditions most closely resemble the early 1990s, which also included a shallow recession. Despite the current recessionary fears, the economy grew early in 2008, although GDP went negative in Q3 2008. Although at this writing it appears the recession will be deeper than the last one in 2002, I don't believe we'll see anything as severe as a depression.

Third, inflation. Think back to early 2008 when oil did the unthinkable: it topped $100 a barrel and kept right on climbing. Average gasoline prices across the United States rose above $3 and then above $4 a gallon. The doomsayers were talking about $200 a barrel oil and gasoline prices that would be $5 a gallon by summer 2008 and on their way to $10. That just didn't happen. All along I suggested that inflated energy prices could not be sustained. The speculative hype just is not there anymore, nor is the demand. We can consume the same amounts of energy and obtain much more output than we have in the past — not just conserving, like going on a short-term diet, but changing the behavior of how we consume. I am not naive enough to assume we can conserve our way into the future; I am just pointing out that the supply and demand curve at the high prices was not sustainable. We can clearly receive more output for the same dollar spent on a unit of energy.

Fourth, housing. Now we come to the trouble spot. Whenever people ask me about housing—particularly if they have a house they need or want to sell—I feel like the proverbial bearer of bad news. Believing it's better to rip off the Band-Aid rather than pull it in small, painful increments, I'm going to give it to you straight: the housing market isn't going back to what it was any time soon. The house you hoped to sell for $300,000, $500,000, $800,000, or whatever isn't going to fetch that much. It may be a little or a lot lower than that depending upon your market.

The problem is one of deleveraging of assets and the lack of liquidity. Deleveraging is just a fancy way of saying that a particular asset—a house, for example—can only be valued based on factors such as the location, size, type of property, and so forth. If this sounds like a return to the good ol' days when a prospective buyer with a down payment in cash met with the local banker to discuss a mortgage, it is. Asset values need to be determined by the marketplace, what is "fair" for a seller to expect and a buyer to pay, given the current conditions and the ability to secure financing in what is admittedly a tougher credit market.

During the housing bubble, however, the value of the asset became immaterial. I'd go so far as to state that the price of the house was not as important as the monthly payment. As long as the payment was "X" per month, nobody cared much about whether the house was priced at $300,000 or $500,000, or some other number. Prices went higher because mortgage rates were low and credit was easy. Sellers got more and buyers bought more, and everybody was happy because housing prices were expected to keep going up. The same was true with other assets that could be leveraged: commercial properties, appliances, automobiles (especially SUVs), computer systems, you name it. The overall price didn't matter, as long as the monthly payment was manageable and the credit terms were liberal.

There are countless stories of homebuyers who were giddy with disbelief that they were able to buy an X-dollar house. They'd leave the bank and the mortgage company with dollar signs in their eyes because they had the buying power to get a much more expensive house than they ever imagined. Now instead of buying a house for "this much," they suddenly could afford a house for "THAT much." What was really happening, however, was all the housing prices had been ratcheted up because of easy lending practices. So a house that went for, say, $500,000 before was suddenly priced at $650,000. And buyers who thought they could only afford the $500,000 house were suddenly able to afford the monthly payment on a house that was selling for $650,000.

The key phase everyone heard during the housing bubble was "stretch." The prevailing advice was "buy a little bigger (newer, fancier, better, more expensive, etc.) than you think, because you'll wish you did later." Then buyers looked at the numbers. If they bought, say, 20 percent more house they'd only be paying $600 more a month, or $20 a day. That became "nothing" to them—just $20 more a day to live in a dream house. Or maybe they were more conservative and decided to buy 10 percent more house for $300 more a month, or $10 a day. Just bringing lunch instead of eating out would make up that difference.

Some buyers stretched and they were fine, even though housing prices have come down. Their monthly mortgage payments are still manageable. Others stretched to the breaking point, and then something snapped. Perhaps they were counting on home prices continuing to climb so they could refinance and pay off debts. Or maybe the numbers just got more "real," that having to pay $2,000 or $3,000 or more a month for a mortgage didn't leave an awful lot left to live on.

Then the bubble burst, the credit market got messy, and the rest as we've discussed already, is history. If we focus on just the impact on homebuyers, however, we only see half the picture. The underlying dynamic in the credit bubble was the ability of banks and mortgage companies to securitize the loans and turn them into a financial instrument that others were willing to buy. So mortgages were bundled together and sold to someone, who carried it as an asset on their balance sheets. It wasn't just the defaults that hurt those mortgage-backed assets.

When the housing market declined in value, suddenly the assets backing those loans fell. The value of the portfolio of loans was less because the assets behind them weren't worth the initial selling price of the homes.

Now the market is trying to define the value of assets that are unlevered. How much is a house worth on its own, without being mortgaged, securitized, bundled with other loans, and sold to a pension fund? My guess is it will take a while for that to be worked out, region by region. A lot of it depends upon the underlying demand that's waiting on the sidelines, the number of properties available, and the overall appeal of location. Unless you are thinking of selling your home right now, this really isn't a problem. My advice would be to stay put and live in your house, as opposed to seeing it as an investment to be bought and sold quickly.

While "paper wealth" isn't real money, consumers do have to adjust to a decline in the wealth effect from the drop in housing prices. It's a proven economic phenomenon that when people feel wealthier—for example, because rising equity prices have swelled the value of their stock portfolios and 401(k) plans—they spend more. With stocks, the behavior and the aftermath is very different than the wealth effect from housing. For example, if you bought a stock for $10 and it rallied all the way to $50, that $50,000 in your account would make you feel $40,000 richer. You might even sell the stock and spend the money, maybe on a sports car. Now if the stock market drops, you might not feel as "wealthy," but you would still own your sports car. You could conceivably sell the car for, say, $30,000 in a year or two and buy the stock back at a lower price and be pretty much back at square one.

The wealth effect in housing was a different matter. People felt wealthier because their $300,000 house was now worth $450,000. Rather than just let the money sit there, they put their equity to work. (And how many times did people hear that message in one form or the other during the credit boom?) So they took out a $100,000 or $150,000 home equity loan and bought two cars, furnished the house, got a sailboat, or some such thing. That home equity loan is not like selling a stock: one transaction and you're done. You didn't saw off the front porch and sell it or reduce the house from four-bedrooms to three. You have a loan that carries compound interest. When home values decline, you suddenly have two mortgages on a piece of property that's worth less. You don't feel as wealthy as you did before when home prices were higher, and you have an extra debt burden.

Where's the Bull?

As lousy as the aforementioned problems are, there is truly a bull inside this bear. I repeat: I believe the next opportunity will be in equities, thanks in part to corporate profits that will drive the stock market higher along with valuations that have become compressed and an economy that, once it hits bottom, will expand and take equities with it. But there are other factors involved, too, including the liquidity in the marketplace meant to address the problems created by the credit crisis.

Just like the "fix" after the tech bubble crash and the liquidity provided in the early 2000s ended up in housing, this time around it will flow to a new location. Yes, as I keep saying, it's the early 1990s all over again. The liquidity to help the banking system after the S&L crisis went into stocks—and in the case of tech stocks inflated a bubble. This time, I believe that the liquidity fix will once again help stock prices.

From a purely cyclical perspective, it's the stock market's turn. For the past eight years or so, the stock market has been pretty lackluster. Even though companies have grown and the economy, for the most part, has expanded, the stock market is roughly flat. As of December 2008, the Dow Jones Industrial Average (DJIA) is above 8,000. For January 2000, the average closing price for the DJIA was 10,900. In order for the stock market to post an average 8 percent annual return year-to-year (as illustrated by the long-term performance of the Dow since 1950 in Figure 7.3 and the Dow's return since 1988 in Figure 7.4), we're going to have to see equities play a game of catch-up.

In other words, it appears that we're in for some overperformance in equities just to have stocks continue to produce an average annual return over the long time that is in line with historical averages.

Beware of Bonds: The Next Bubble to Burst

As recent history has shown us, the way to fix one broken bubble is to create another one, which would last a little bit longer and take a few

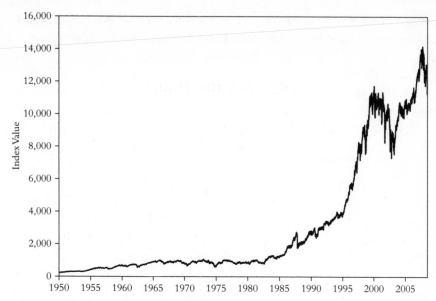

Figure 7.3   Dow Jones Industrial Average Performance Since 1950
SOURCE: Dow Jones & Company: www.djindexes.com.

Figure 7.4   Dow Jones Industrial Average Performance Since 1988
SOURCE: Dow Jones & Company: www.djindexes.com.

more investors along for the ride. As we've seen, recent bubbles were caused by excessive liquidity and the flawed concept that valuation didn't matter—plus, an unhealthy dose of the belief that trees really can grow to the sky.

When the twin bubbles in housing and credit burst, the first casualties were the sophisticated debt instruments such as collateralized debt obligations (CDOs), collateralized mortgage obligations (CMOs), as well as a host of other acronym-named instruments. When the bubbles burst, the assets that backed these notes declined sharply. These fancy securities that had looked so good on paper in the days of easy money depreciated just like a high-flying Internet stock that was shot down when the tech bubble burst.

In hindsight, it was easy to see that some of those Internet stocks (no earnings and hardly any revenues to speak of) were doomed from the start. The same applies to these sophisticated debt assets as well. However, the fallout from the debt instruments is much larger than the debris from the tech stock implosion. The reason is the size of the debt instrument market dwarfed that of initial public offerings (IPOs), which had launched so many of those Internet high-flyers. Additionally, these instruments were posted as collateral to borrow even more money to buy even more debt instruments.

So how to fix the problem of the debt instrument crisis, which has wreaked havoc in the marketplace and on banks' balance sheets? As discussed in Chapter 6, the Federal Reserve has already adopted an accommodative stance. With the Federal Funds rates below 50 basis points (as of December 2008), it's not like there is much more we can do. While the existing liquidity will help fuel the next expansion (as stated before, in equities), where will be the next bubble to inflate as investors desperately seek a balloon to grab onto now that easy access to credit has disappeared?

This time the bubble will be the bubble machine itself. The entire credit market was levered, hedged, or traded against U.S. Treasuries. Spreads, as they are called, allowed the marketplace to evaluate the risk of credit securities. It started as hedges against mortgages. Risk was measured by the spread relationship, which traded in a nice, orderly range. As foreign demand for securities increased, helping to push rates lower, it encouraged or at least provided an incentive for borrowers to take on more debt. We borrowed against our greatest assets—our homes—and more importantly we consumed the amount that we borrowed. We spent borrowed money with the expectation that the underlying assets (our homes) would appreciate in value as we purchased depreciating goods and services—many of them from foreign countries. Our spending on foreign goods and services increased the U.S. trade deficit and filled coffers overseas with dollars that were used in turn to purchase our debt. That demand for debt pushed Treasuries even higher and rates lower. And this gave borrowers the ability to borrow even more and buy still more foreign goods, and so the cycle continued. It looked like a win-win, as long as the assets that backed consumers' borrowing kept rising in value, lenders were able to hedge, and the spread remained stable.

Then the bubble burst in housing and the credit market headed south on a wave of subprime losses.

Now the next bubble is the last leg of trade positions in Treasuries. As the hedge actually lost money and positions became worthless, investors, pension funds, money managers, and others headed for the safety of the most liquid and secure market in the world: the U.S. bond market. This buying pushed prices up and yields down to levels equivalent to the recession days of earlier in this decade. Initially, more Fed easing helped calm investors' nerves as lower rates supported higher prices. Then, demand from investors that shunned any other type of security as being too risky has poured in the Treasury market. The final blast to inflate this bubble came as all the positions that had used Treasury bonds, notes, or bills to hedge against some asset-backed security (CDOs, CMOs, etc.), which are now worthless, were still buying hedges. This last event is causing a bubble to develop because it is occurring with little regard to fundamentals. So why have yields been the same or lower? (See Figure 7.5.)

Soon we will see investors begin to lose money by investing in Treasuries. With yields below the rate of inflation, real returns are negative. Once the bubble pops, bond prices will decline, causing a capital loss that will resemble the bond market debacle from earlier in this decade.

At some point the gobs of cash that have been rushing into bonds will venture out ever so slowly into riskier investments. Not the high-yield stuff that burned everyone, but high-grade, good quality stuff that survived this contraction. That will be the first sign, as this initial selling

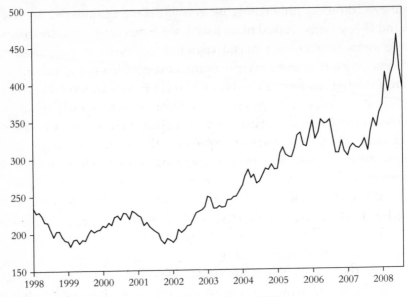

Figure 7.5   Reuters/Jefferies CRB Index Since 1998
SOURCE: Commodity Research Bureau.

will cause yields to rise and prices to fall. Then rates will be forced higher as more capital is needed to address the various problems from the financial sector, both public and private. This competition for capital will put even more upward pressure on rates.

Finally, the banking system will be saved by the same plan that bailed out the S&L crisis. Long-term rates will be pushed artificially higher, well beyond inflation and GDP growth, and short-term rates will remain low compared to economic fundamentals. Banks and financial institutions will be encouraged to borrow short term at low rates and loan longer term at rates that are higher than Treasury notes, bonds, and bills (as well as some very high-quality corporate borrowers).

A variety of forces will come together to make the perfect storm to pop the bond market bubble. Shorts that hedged will finally cover. Fundamentals will create an outflow of money, as investors will not accept negative real returns. More bonds will be issued to pay for the financial mess, thus increasing the supply of bonds—which will need higher rates to attract capital. Lastly, the Fed will eventually try to create a very steep and positively sloped yield curve to clean up the balance sheets of banks and other institutions. In advance of this storm hitting the bond market, we all need to monitor how to clean up our balance sheets and deleverage investment portfolios.

The previous scenario pinpoints the next bubble to pop, with a bear market contraction to begin in bonds. One of the contributing factors— a positive yield curve—is generally considered positive for the economy and for the stock market. That further supports the next bull to emerge in the overall economy and the broader equity markets, ushering in a period of overperformance for perhaps the next five to ten years.

The Bull Inside the Bear: Reverting to the Mean

Over time, every real asset reverts to its mean. By real asset, I mean those that have a recognized valuation over time; for example, commodities, real estate, and stocks of companies that have a track record of earnings. A dot-com stock in the midst of the late-1990s craze was not a real asset. When those stocks went down 50 percent or more, there was no reverting to the mean, because the valuation had been all based on perception—not reality.

Therefore, one opportunity in equities will be as the broader market reverts back to its mean. Because of the lackluster performance over the past eight years, there will be acceleration to the upside. Now, I'm not suggesting that you jump into leveraged options and futures in order to make up for lost time in the stock market. Rather, I'm suggesting that, where equities are concerned, it soon will be time to get back into the water.

Admittedly this is against the grain for many people who still remember getting burned when tech stocks went down in flames. After seeing account statements go from positive to negative, they swore off equities. And there are many people out there who think that we're in for a very rough ride, economically speaking.

What we're experiencing right now is what's typical during periods of contraction. Assets that have been overvalued (housing) snap back to more rational levels. The more out of line those assets were on the upside, the longer it takes for things to get normal again. And we could see some overreaction on the downside as well, particularly if sellers panic.

As we work our way through the problems and with the strong hand of the Fed on the rudder, the stage is set for the next expansion (bull market) to occur in equities. When, it is hard to say exactly. As of this writing, 2009 looks a bit mixed as the aftermath of the current troubles continues. But by late 2009 we should be at the start of a new expansion phase in equities, and headed for a good year in 2010. To go out on a limb, I'd say by the time this book is published (spring 2009), we should have seen the bottom and will already be turning to the upside.

Let's Talk Game Plan

Remember, one of the first opportunities for the bull inside the bear is going to be to recapture lost ground. Assets that have been oversold will eventually move higher as they revert back to the mean. One of the sectors that I believe should be closely watched is the financials (see Figure 7.6).

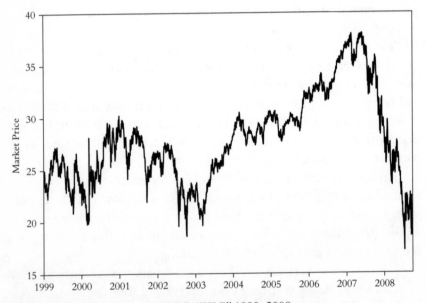

Figure 7.6   Financial Sector SPDR "XLF" 1999–2008
SOURCE: Reproduced with permission of Yahoo! Inc. ® 2008 by Yahoo! Inc. YAHOO! and the YAHOO! logo are trademarks of Yahoo! Inc.

The financial stocks have seen a sharp decline, with continued pressure due to the credit crisis, concern over more mortgage defaults, and the effect of a weaker economy. I don't believe whatever bad news comes next will be enough to knock this sector down another 50 percent. And even if the financials do take it on the chin, I doubt they will have a devastating impact on the broader market or the economy as a whole.

Therefore, one place I would look to invest in over the coming months would be the banking and financial sector. I suggest nibbling at first and then diving into banks and financials once employment trends reverse to the upside in this sector. Do not overweight this sector, however, as the higher interest rates will be a drag. But as it returns to its normal functioning there should be plenty of opportunity during the initial phase as these proven assets with long track records revert to the mean. There will be a lot of lost ground to recover—let alone any potential upside for the long-term. Rather than pick one or two stocks, however, I would advise investing more broadly through ETFs. As we'll discuss in an upcoming chapter, with ETFs investors can take advantage of broad market or sector movements, without having to pick individual stocks. The ETF for the financial sector is XLF—but remember, just a small position as this sector has been badly damaged.

In addition to the financial sector, investors would do well to establish positions in the broader indexes, again using ETFs such as: the S&P 500 (ETF symbol SPY); Nasdaq (ETF symbol QQQQ), as technology usually leads the market out of contraction; and what I personally feel will be the strongest risk adjusted and least volatile performer, the Russell 2000 (IWM).

Doubling the Dow

From wherever the low point is in the DJIA I would expect it to double within five or so years. Absent any *new* problems (and with the old and lingering ones getting cleaned up over time) I believe that could easily be accomplished. If you look at recent history, from the October 2002 low of 7,200, the DJIA doubled to 14,000 in July 2007—just a little under five years.

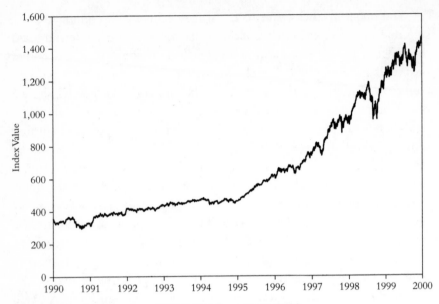

Figure 7.7   Performance of S&P 500 from 1990–2000
Source: Standard & Poor's (S&P): Central Inquiry Office; Moody's Economy.com.

So when should you get in? What I'm talking about is the potential for a long cycle. Getting in at the bottom or being "early" doesn't mean as much as investing in the direction of the overall trend. As we saw in the 1990s, while the S&Ps tripled or even quadruped by 2000 (see Figure 7.7), even if you didn't get in until the trend was well under way—say, in 1995 or so—you still would have doubled your money.

As of this publication date, I'd say it was time to dip a toe into the investment water. You don't have to go all the way in at this point. Making quarterly or monthly investments is a good way to start. That way you will have a variety of entry prices which, over time, will give you an average basis that is not dependent upon picking the absolute bottom or picking the top like in bonds that will trend lower as yields normalize. I would sell out of fixed income assets and low yielding money markets and make larger investments in the equity markets trying to diversify among noncorrelating sectors (which you'll read more about in the ETF chapter).

So my advice:

- Don't take out a second mortgage or put any more debt on your home.
- Don't speculate on housing, even if it is cheap and looks attractive.
- Empty the mattress and get your money out of the perceived safety of money markets and Treasuries.
- Step in with one toe in the equity market, using exchange-traded funds to gain exposure to positively sloped sectors.
- And always look for the bull inside the bear.

Part III

INVESTMENT LESSONS TO LIVE BY

Chapter 8

ETFs

The Perfect Investment

Wlabelhen most people want to get into the stock market, what action do they take? Often they choose a mutual fund, based on a variety of criteria, from the returns they saw advertised someplace to the risk/reward rating in the financial pages. Or perhaps they try their hand at the stock-picking game, trying to determine which issue is not only going in the same direction as the overall market, but is likely to outperform as well. It may be that an investor has done some research, or perhaps has followed Peter Lynch's fabled advice to accompany teenagers to the mall and notice where and what they buy—and then select stocks accordingly. Or they may get a tip from somebody about what makes Company X such a great buy.

To capture the opportunity for the next bull inside the bear in the equities market, which could see a doubling of the Dow from wherever it puts in a low in the late 2008 to early 2009 time frame, I would suggest a new tactic: the exchange-traded fund (ETF).

As you've probably gathered by now, I am a big fan of the ETF. An ETF is a type of security that represents an index or a basket of stocks. This is a generic term, with particular ETFs offered under a variety of names and by different market players. Using an ETF, you can make an investment in a specific sector or broad index just as easily as you could buy shares in IBM or Microsoft.

Exchange-traded funds are so revolutionary, I believe everyone should use them, whether money manager or individual investor, in order to gain exposure to indices and sectors. For example, if you want to invest in the broad market such as the Standard & Poor's 500 Index, there are ETFs for that (such as SPDRs or "spiders" as they're called). You think energy stocks are going up? You can buy the XLE. Financial stocks? The XLF. Name an index, a sector, or a segment, and it's more than likely that there's a correlating ETF.

As we'll discuss in this chapter, ETFs offer ease and flexibility to take advantage of growth and expansion in particular sectors or the broad market. At the same time, they have certain defensive qualities that enhance their applicability, particularly in the midst of market uncertainty.

An Investment for Uncertain Times

When turmoil hits the market such as we've seen in the second half of 2008, I am frequently asked—no, actually, I'm begged—for advice on where investors can hide. As we've seen in late 2008, stocks are down in some cases more than 20 percent, commodities are down similarly, and energy is also off sharply. High-grade bonds are being trashed and are down as much as stocks. Even cash in banks is viewed as shaky given the condition of some of the larger institutions. And as for real estate, it has turned into the proverbial roach motel: you can't finance, refinance, or sell it, so once you check into that investment, you can't check out.

As of this writing, blue chip stocks are down across the board and some also appear to be headed the way of some of the banks. Many foreign markets have declined as much as the U.S. equity markets. Overseas markets that have not fallen as much appeared ready to take the plunge.

What this points to is a portfolio of diversified ETFs. Not only can a portfolio of ETFs be constructed to perform in all types of market conditions, but they also provide many other safety features as well. One advantage of ETFs, which has nothing to do with a particular investment strategy, is that these securities are held in your name—not the name of the institution. Thus, they are insulated from the financial conditions of the brokerage firm. In fact, in the "olden days," you didn't even need a brokerage account to hold them because they were actually delivered as certificates with the owner's name neatly etched on them.

Second, ETFs replicate indexes or sectors that may include, in some cases, hundreds of stocks. Even if a company here or there goes to zero, the index will not. Yes, an ETF can see a downward move of 20 percent or more, just like the overall market, but the likelihood of an ETF going to zero is very remote, if not mathematically impossible. For example, the ETF for the financial sector is the XLF. Even though this sector has been under pressure given the credit and liquidity crises, the ground zero of the current mess is not at "zero." Even when the XLF was down 30 percent or so, it was a far better investment than an individual stock such as Lehman Brothers, Bear Stearns, or Wachovia—and the XLF pays a 4 percent dividend to boot. Admittedly, a 20 to 30 percent loss is painful, but it's not a goose egg. My point here is not to recommend the XLF or any specific ETF, but to show that the structure of these investments is attractive for those wishing to "take cover."

Additionally, ETFs track everything from metals to energy to fixed income. There are also inverse ETFs that allow you to buy a position that replicates being short a particular sector, index, or the overall market. As a basket of holdings, an ETF may be easier to add to or subtract from a portfolio than a single instrument. For example, the ETF "SHY" is comprised of short-term government bonds, and is easier to sell than an individual bond. At the same time, the SHY combines several short-term maturities in one instrument and can be bought and sold like a stock. And, as stated before, it is kept in your name. That means no matter what else fails, your portfolio is still *your* portfolio.

Stock pickers are very talented and possess a skill set I never had, but in a meltdown environment all stocks get hit—even the good ones. There are examples of very well-run companies whose stock price is in the single digits, and even those that have been forced to merge, sell, or go out of business. But I have never heard of an index or ETF going out of business (delisting doesn't count). In fact, during the bear market and contraction of 2001 to 2003, many sectors doubled or tripled while the economy faltered and the S&P lost 50 percent and tech stocks plummeted 75 percent.

Using ETFs also gives you the ability to hedge your portfolio by buying inverse instruments, which go up in value when the market or index goes down. You could even create a no risk portfolio of longs and shorts using ETFs that will insulate you from market meltdowns and have the security of knowing you can liquidate at anytime regardless of the strength of a particular institution.

I am not saying that ETFs will protect you from losing money, as that simply is not true. Risk is a factor in any investment plan. However, ETFs give investors the tools to create a diversified portfolio of specific sectors including bonds and inverse products, which in times of concern can provide a sense of security and confidence that can never be achieved with individual stocks.

For example, during September 29, 2008—the day the Dow had its largest one-day drop of 777 points—almost 499 out of 500 stocks were down. The exception? Campell Soup Company, which led to some speculation that investors were either seeking the comfort of a hot bowl of soup—or those with the bunker mentality were stocking up on canned goods. Or take a look at the week ending October 2, 2008, one of the worst weeks ever for the market, with the S&P 500 down more than 9 percent, the Nasdaq Composite off more than 10 percent, and the Dow nearly 10 percent lower. A quick view of the ETF universe revealed 20 ETFs that were actually *up* that week. Yes, some were inverse or bond-related, but up is up, and defense can be played with a single trade or two or mouse click away.

Perhaps the safety features of an ETF portfolio make it sound like an Armageddon strategy—like finding a cave and stocking it with canned goods, water, and guns. If so, it may be. But imagine the portfolios you can build 80 percent of the time when we are in a normal, positively sloped market environment somewhere. Using ETFs would be a more efficient way to build a portfolio that has a greater probability of achieving average or above average returns with less risk hassle and aggravation.

Using ETFs

The American Stock Exchange, which pioneered the creation of the ETF, today lists more than 200 ETFs. Barclay's iShares also offers ETFs in a variety of sectors and indices. All in all, there are hundreds of ETFs available: broad market, large cap, mid cap, and small cap; specific sectors, such as healthcare and technology; as well as real estate, international, fixed income, commodities, and a specialty category of very specific offerings. In general, they are highly liquid and easy to buy and sell—just like a stock.

There are several advantages ETFs have over mutual funds, including the ability to enter and exit a position at any time, and not just at the end of the trading day, as well as lower fees and associated costs compared to mutual funds. Plus ETFs are a pure play, meaning you're buying exposure to a basket of stocks that represent an index or sector. You're not buying a mutual fund that tracks a particular index—along with whatever spin the fund manager can put on the ball in order to differentiate his or her track record from the pack. Since the vast majority of fund managers do not beat their benchmarks, many investors choose to invest in the benchmark. With ETFs you can easily gain exposure to indices such as the S&P 500, Nasdaq, Russell 2000, or others, as a pure play, without the manager's attempt to finesse returns.

If you want to invest in technology, an ETF will give you exposure to a basket of technology stocks. With a mutual fund, you are also subject to the discretion of the manager who may decide that Apple Computer is a better pick than Dell, or vice versa. The fund's performance will be higher or lower versus the sector in aggregate based on whether the manager was right. Or maybe a fund has an automotive specialty, but there could be quite a bit of leeway in the stocks selected beyond the typical Ford or General Motors. A fund manager could make a case for this, including Goodyear (tires) or maybe BP Amoco (fuel). But at some point, the industry exposure that you hoped to gain through a fund could be diluted by how far the manager expands the investment theme.

With ETFs, you have exposure to a particular sector or index—period. And you can easily find out just what holdings are in any ETF by using tools such as Yahoo Finance or a new free information and education web site launched by my firm, www.etfport.com.

The ETF Advantage

- Pure play in index or sector
- The ability to buy and sell shares just like a stock
- Lower fees and related expenses versus mutual funds
- Highly liquid markets
- Widely available information on pricing, sector components, and so forth
- Diversification across multiple industries, sectors and indices, even for relatively small portfolios
- Long and short positions can be established easily
- Lower volatility based on performance of a group of stocks or index versus a single security

ETF Innovation

I'm such a fan of the ETF, I truly believe that this is the *greatest financial innovation since the creation of the put*! Now those are pretty strong words. Allow me to explain. Back in the early days of options, there were only calls, which give the buyer the right (but not the obligation) to take a long position in the underlying security. Calls worked great if you thought the underlying market or security was going up, but if you wanted to be short, you were more or less out of luck. (Yes, you could write calls, which would allow you to retain the premium if the market went down, but your potential risk exposure was far greater than just being able to take a short position.)

With the creation of the put, it was now possible to establish a short position using options, and risk only the premium paid. This was a major innovation in financial securities that helped to revolutionize investing. By using the put, investors and speculators can take advantage of downward moves while limiting their capital-at-risk to the premium paid.

I believe that ETFs give investors the same degree of fire power when it comes to executing their investment decisions. Exchange-traded funds allow investors to have both short and long positions—easily and without the need to short stocks—as well as to gain specific sector exposure.

If my glowing praise about ETFs isn't enough to convince you, here's my personal testimony. My firm, Astor Financial LLC, implements our investment strategies largely using ETFs, along with some futures and options. The reason is, as an economist, I look at the big picture first to determine the overall trend of the economy. As previously stated, the four cycles of the economy—expansion, peak, contraction, and trough—are identifiable with certain characteristics. In an expansion phase, for example, I want to have exposure to a broad market index such as the S&P or the Dow. I can accomplish this with an ETF. Further, if I see growth in a particular industry that may very well indicate expansion that is outpacing the overall economy. If so, I may want to invest in that sector through a more targeted ETF. Whatever my investment hypothesis based on my economic analysis, there is an ETF that allows me to put my ideas into action.

My economist's approach works very well in conjunction with an investment vehicle such as the ETF because I'm not a stock analyst. If you want to know why Microsoft should be trading at $28 and not $25 (or whatever the numbers), I'm not the guy to ask. In fact, I'm always amazed at how much variation there can be in valuations of a company such as Pepsico. No matter how big the firm or how many analysts are following it, you can get a great deal of divergence of opinion when it comes to valuation.

I don't believe that stock picking is an efficient way to invest, especially for the individual investor, and thankfully I don't have to engage in that type of analysis since it's not my strong suit. The expertise I've honed over the years is studying the economy for signs and confirmation of its current phase (expansion, peak, contraction, or trough) and to invest accordingly. I'm much more comfortable with a long-term horizon, noticing what's going, and then making investment decisions based on particular economic fundamentals, whether a certain sector is adding jobs or there has been an uptick in demand for a certain kind of product. The sector approach works well for me versus getting pinned down to a specific price target for a particular stock, based on certain information such as an earnings miss or an upside surprise.

Plus there is the chance that even if you had the overall market trend right and the correct sector spotlighted, you could pick the wrong stock. Maybe you think the transportation sector is going to be strong. As you look at possible investment candidates, you pick Company A. The overall sector goes up by a double-digit percentage, but Company A only moves a few percentage points, or maybe it goes down. The reason may be anything from another business line that's suffering to fundamental problems at the company. Any number of reasons can explain why a particular stock doesn't perform like the rest of its peers.

Granted, by investing in a sector using an ETF, instead of picking individual stocks, you will miss the opportunity to get onboard with that one, rare superstar that outperforms all the rest. At the same time, you'll miss the impact of the laggard that goes south while the rest of the flock heads north. With an ETF you will reap the aggregate performance of the group. Further, because you're buying shares in a basket of stocks or indexes, volatility will be lower than if you picked just one stock. If we all agree that more is better than less and diversification is the key ingredient to an efficient and productive portfolio, then ETFs trump stock picking by a landslide. Not only do ETFs trade like a stock but each ETF share represents dozens and in some cases, hundreds, of stocks. Now that is true diversification, and potentially with some tax advantages to boot.

As an economist and money manager, I'd rather focus on GDP output, employment levels, and other economic indicators. Once I determine that the broad market or certain sectors should go in a particular direction, I invest accordingly, staying the course until some fundamental changes occur.

A sector doesn't need a price target; it can expand until it doesn't anymore. As for price-to-earnings (P/E) ratios, they seem to go from overvalued to undervalued for reasons that seem to be completely arbitrary. It appears that during expansions P/E ratios get overvalued and continue to get overvalued until the economy changes and then stocks correct, at which point the P/Es contract until they are undervalued and continue to get more undervalued until the economy starts to expand. So why try to measure the temperature in winter hoping for a sunny 80-degree day, when you're better off waiting until summer? As for me, I don't worry about the readings at all. I make my decisions based on economic fundamentals, and then ETFs allow me to execute quickly, easily, and in virtually any position size.

Using ETFs, investors can gain exposure to a wide variety of indices and sectors. A small, random sampling includes:

Aerospace and Defense	Oil Services
Agriculture	Pharmaceutical
Base Metals	Retail
Basic Materials	Semiconductors
Consumer Discretionary	Software
Food and Beverage	Transportation

Pure Investment, No Ego

With an ETF, you're making your decisions without specific names attached to it. You're picking the "financial sector," not XYZ Financial Inc. Your choice is "technology stocks," not ABC Super-Fast Chips.

With an ETF you are buying the index. Period. That's why I consider an ETF a "no-ego" investment. Your investment bet is on a particular group of stocks—whether to the upside or the downside—not on the fact that you think there's a bunch of whiz kids running the show someplace.

Therefore, if there is a drawback at all to investing in ETFs versus picking stocks, it is a psychological one. When you buy shares of, say, IBM or General Electric, you are in effect the owner of a tiny "piece" of the company. That is, after all, the purpose of the stock market, which does not exist in order to provide a platform for speculators. Rather, the stock market is a mechanism for companies to raise capital from investors. Even as an individual shareholder, you know (at least in theory) that the company management and the board of directors are answerable to you.

This thinking is aligned with the prevalent Wall Street culture, which is research- and trading-related. A Wall Street analyst or a large investor is introduced to the CEO, hears a presentation about the company, and undertakes research on some facet of the business, from its new product launches to its inventory management systems. There are certainly a lot of research firms that sell their stock analysis, as well as investors who are eager to buy information on new, unknown companies that promise to be the next Starbucks or Home Depot.

Institutional investors set the tone for the investing public, who want to hear from the CEO (whether in person or in an interview with CNBC) about how the company is going to sell 100 more widgets this year than last year, and do so at a lower cost.

An ETF will not give you that satisfaction of ownership. And you won't be cheering for "your" management team as it (hopefully) beats the competition, and you won't get invited to the annual meeting. You will, however, gain the benefit of the aggregate performance of all the stocks in a particular sector or index, however narrow or wide.

ETFs for Retirement Plans

Exchange-traded funds also expand the menu of choices offered in many company-sponsored 401(k) plans. In the past, employees were given a limited number of mutual funds to choose from: usually, big cap, small cap, value, growth, fixed income, and maybe international. Now plans are offering more product choices, including ETFs and certain annuity products.

If you participate in a company 401(k) plan, find out what investment choices are being offered. If your company does not offer ETFs, contact human resources to inquire about adding in that option.

Exchange-traded funds can enhance returns and give you the ability to execute an investment strategy based on your analysis, with exposure to certain segments at the most opportune time.

Thinking Like an Economist

Investing in an ETF means you're thinking like an economist most of the time, instead of a Wall Street stock picker. You're making decisions such as: *I see that demand for infrastructure stocks given the Obama stimulus package is increasing at such a rate that I believe the basic materials sector will grow exponentially.* Your investment decision is based on the belief that the sector as a whole will show greater market share and improved profitability, regardless of how each individual player performs.

Another way to look at ETFs is as a way to participate in certain investment opportunities without the physical aspect to it. Back in the days of the housing boom and bubble, if you thought property values were going to skyrocket, you didn't have to go through all the trouble of buying a house, renovating it, and flipping it in a quick sale. You could have bought a real estate ETF, gained exposure to the sector, and made a profit. No need to hire a contractor or hold Sunday afternoon open houses for prospective buyers. You could get in and out of the investment quickly and easily.

The same could be said for any commodity, from agricultural products to precious metals. Rather than investment in the physical material (e.g., buying gold or silver coins) or, to take this to an extreme, renting some farmland and planting a crop, there's an ETF with your desired name on it.

When it comes to tapping the investment opportunity of a particular sector I can think of no better example than energy (except that it has been cited ad nauseum). The bull market in energy coincided with a bear market/contraction in the broader market, such as the S&P 500. Seeing the rise in energy prices, you could have broad exposure to the sector through the energy sector ETF, such as the XLE (see Figure 8.1). With

Figure 8.1 Energy ETF "XLE" (Solid Line) vs. S&P ETF "SPY" (Dotted Line) October 2006–September 2008

one security, you could have participated in the overall performance of stocks such as ExxonMobil, Chevron, ConocoPhillips, Schlumberger, Occidental Petroleum, Devon Energy, Transocean, Apache Corporation, National Oilwell Varco, Hess Corporation, and others.

The bottom line is, with ETFs you gain exposure to baskets of stocks that may have a few dozen issues in them or several hundred. That provides a level of diversification that is simply not possible to achieve by the average investor with a brokerage account. Even with a relatively small amount of money, say $10,000 or $20,000, you could parlay that into exposure in hundreds or even thousands of stocks across various asset classes: small cap, large cap, broad market, sectors—all by buying shares in a few ETFs.

Going Short by Going Long

As mentioned earlier, inverse ETFs offer investors the ability to have a short position in the market without having to sell short. For example, if you think that the Nasdaq is due for a correction, you can buy shares of an inverse ETF known as the QID. When the value of the Nasdaq index declines, the QID goes up in price.

There are inverse ETFs that replicate a short position in many of the major indices and sectors, from the S&P to financial stocks. In addition, many ETFs offer double exposure—long or short—to a particular index, giving you the potential (if you're right about the trend) to "super-size" your return.

To illustrate, here's what taking a short position in the financial stocks via an ultra-short financial ETF known as SKF would have done for you from May to July 2008, at a time when financial institutions were under pressure post-credit crisis, as illustrated in Figure 8.2.

The innovation of the inverse ETF is nothing short of a breakthrough for investors who want to speculate in the downward movements of a market or sector, but do not feel comfortable shorting a stock. Back in the early days of my firm, we wanted to go short during the recession of 2001. Because inverse ETFs hadn't been launched yet, we had to short sell the SPDR (the S&P ETF) and the QQQQ (the Nasdaq ETF). The expansion of ETF offerings has allowed investment firms

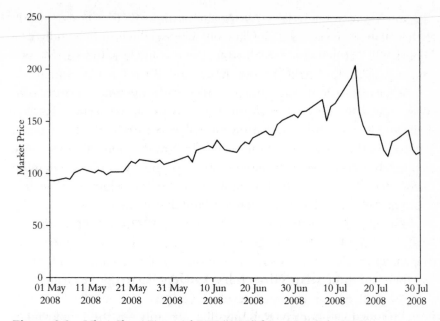

Figure 8.2   Ultra-Short Financial ETF "SKF" from May–July 2008
SOURCE: Reproduced with permission of Yahoo! Inc. ® 2008 by Yahoo! Inc. YAHOO! and the
YAHOO! logo are trademarks of Yahoo! Inc.

such as Astor to develop and execute strategies easily and in highly liquid
securities.

Choosing Sectors

The ETFs that you choose to buy will depend, obviously, on your view
of the market at the time. If you think the overall market is expanding,
you can buy an ETF that gives you broad equity exposure such as the
SPDRs (S&P 500) or the DIA "diamonds" (Dow). When it comes to
specific sectors, you can narrow your focus, from buying the QQQQ
to gain exposure to the Nasdaq, to more specific ETFs that provide
industry-focused exposure such as biotechnology, food and beverage,
hardware, insurance, media, pharmaceuticals, and utilities. Sector selection
can get very specific, especially in terms of geographic investment. Here
investors need to ask themselves when a focus becomes too narrow.
While you may consider Argentina to be a hot market for investment,

do you really want to own an Argentina-only ETF? Or would you rather have exposure to Latin America in general or more broadly to a global ETF? If global is too broad and one country is too narrow, you might consider an EAFE (Europe, Australia, and Far East) investment.

Whatever you choose, you can tailor your investment portfolio to your style, whether growth or value, and focus on the sectors that you believe are most in favor. You no longer have to rely on the standard mutual fund choices of big cap/small cap, growth, and value to create a portfolio. With even a relatively small amount, you can accomplish broad diversification, and also home in on certain industries or sectors that you believe to have the strongest growth potential.

This is the same strategy that we employ at Astor, using economic analysis as the basis of our investment strategy to pick the direction of the move (bullish or bearish). Then using certain economic indicators, we focus on those sectors that stand to see the biggest price change.

As we'll discuss in more detail in Chapter 9, one of the indicators that we use—but not the only one, certainly—is the Employment Situation Report, which is released the first Friday of every month. Using the report, we look at individual sectors listed in the report to see which have had significant gains or losses in jobs. For example, in August 2008, the unemployment rate rose to 6.1 percent, the highest rate in nearly five years. In spite of the overall decline in employment, certain sectors did gain jobs. A snapshot from the Employment Situation Report (as shown in Table 8.1) shows some of the job growth.

Looking over the months included in the Employment Report data, you can see the trends in job creation, indicating growth in a particular sector. You can do this analysis on your own—or you can see how we do it via our new web site, www.etfport.com, which offers free information about ETFs, a searchable index of ETFs, and an overview of our economic analysis to use as a guideline to selecting ETFs.

The popularity of the ETF as an investment vehicle has created demand for information. Average investors want to know what ETFs exists, and also the difference between ETFs that offer the same or similar market exposure. For this reason, my firm launched ETF Port (www. etfport.com) as a free portal. The ETF Port's lofty goal is to provide the web's best ETF specific search, research, rankings, and articles. The fund families have wonderful sites, but limit your search to their ETFs. Other

Table 8.1 Employment Report Sector Snapshot (Seasonally Adjusted)

Industry	Sept 07	May 08	June 08	July 08	Aug 08	Sept 08	Change from Aug 08–Sept 08
Total nonfarm	137,837	137,717	137,617	137,550	137,477	137,318	−159
Natural resources and mining	727	760	768	777	789	798	9
Construction	7,589	7,246	7,196	7,173	7,160	7,125	−35
Manufacturing	13,822	13,571	13,527	13,487	13,431	13,380	−51
Trade, transportation, and utilities	26,649	26,451	26,431	26,393	26,356	26,298	−58
Financial activities	8,294	8,226	8,213	8,206	8,201	8,184	−17
Education and health services	18,451	18,820	18,891	18,935	18,994	19,019	25
Leisure and hospitality	13,552	13,679	13,679	13,655	13,645	13,628	−17

Source: Bureau of Labor Statistics, "The Employment Situation: September 2008."

sites might supply articles or research, but not both. The ETF Port is the web's most comprehensive place for ETF research and ideas.

As managers who use ETFs, we would often become interested in a specific sector based on a data point such as employment, and then have a difficult time finding the ETF that tracked that sector. We couldn't help wondering, if we are professionals who understand ETFs and know what we are looking for and still have trouble finding it, how can the average investor be faring? Most research sites require that you know the ticker to research an ETF. Type in a sector such as "energy" or a keyword such as "wind" and the search comes up blank. At ETF Port, you can search either by ticker, keyword, holding, or sector. A search for "wind" takes you to the ETF aptly called FAN. Type in GOOG and you won't get a chart of Google as you would at every other investment site, you'll get a list of ETFs that count Google as one of their top 10 holdings.

Ideas are key to any investor. ETF Port generates articles regularly including profiles on new ETFs, comparisons of ETFs that track the same sector, ideas on new ways to use ETFs in your portfolio, ETFs that could profit based on economic trends, and ETF moves based on technical analysis.

We even provide some of Astor Financial's (my financial services company) "secret sauce ingredients" for investing, such as both fundamental and technical rankings for each ETF and a signals program where each ETF generates a buy, sell, or hold signal at the close of each trading day along with a price target and stop.

Our goal in creating www.etfport.com is to provide information to help people connect the dots to their own investment decisions.

On the Radar for 2009

As of this writing, it's hard to call the market too specifically. As you'll read in Chapter 9, staying nimble by continuously evaluating economic and financial data will help you significantly with your investment choices. The days of "buy and hold and forget about it" are long over. The educated investor watches the economic cycles, including the developments that happen—industry-to-industry—within a cycle.

Since I'm not in the business of picking tops and bottoms in the market, I won't prognosticate as to when I think we'll see the end of the stock market correction. However, I will say that, by the time this book is published in spring 2009, I would expect that an expansion in the broad equity market will be under way already, or will start shortly.

As that happens, there will be sectors on my radar screen.

- **Financials—Beaten Up and Reverting to the Mean:** Financial stocks have been under serious pressure due to the credit crisis. At some point these assets with a long track record will reach the bottom of what has been a severe correction, and start to regain lost ground. By the time you read this book, it's possible that move will already be under way. I would expect at least a 50 percent move off the lows in the financial sector as the assets revert to the mean.
- **Russell—Big Hopes for Small Companies:** One area that is likely to see strong growth is small cap. I do not think that the economic

challenges related to the subprime mess, such as restrictions on overnight borrowing, will affect the smaller companies the way it may hamper the bigger firms. Smaller companies that are in good financial shape are going to benefit more as the economy improves than bigger companies, which may be just as healthy. Therefore, I would recommend exposure to the Russell 2000.

- **Technology—Worth Watching but Beware:** My gut instinct is that technology should be worth watching, but whether it will see a strong uptick in 2009 is uncertain at this point. The theme I would expect for 2009 is reversion, as undervalued assets rise back toward the mean. Technology is often one of the areas to benefit the most as the economy improves. Whether that's a late 2009 or 2010 story is uncertain. My advice at this point is to keep technology on the radar and look for signs of increased orders.

The Bull Inside the Bear: See the Forest, Focus on the Trees

No matter what the investment landscape looks like this year, next year, or beyond, it's important to distinguish between the broad market and individual sectors. In other words, while you're looking at the forest make sure you also notice the trees. If you asked anyone about the stock market in 2008 there wouldn't be much disagreement in their evaluations of a down market—although they may describe it as "awful," "dismal," or some other unpleasant adjective. But not every sector has performed badly.

By second quarter 2008, with the overall market down, the transportation sector was doing well. Now that may seem counterintuitive given the high fuel prices, but the iShares Dow Jones Transportation Average ETF (IYT) was up 19.7 percent for the year-to-date. However, such gains are hardly surprising given that the employment report for January 2008 showed growth in the sector, with jobs being added overall in transportation during November 2007, a trend that was confirmed by positive job growth throughout the first quarter of 2008. As this employment trend indicated, the IYT did outperform the broad market during the first two quarters of 2008, as illustrated in Figure 8.3.

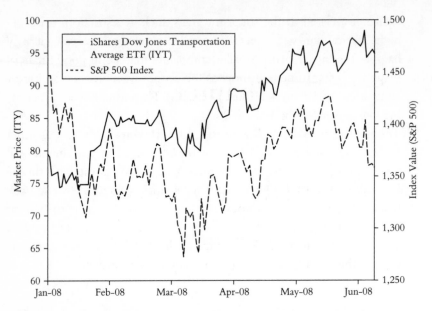

Figure 8.3   Transportation ETF "IYT" January to Mid-June 2008

SOURCE: Reproduced with permission of Yahoo! Inc. ® 2008 by Yahoo! Inc. YAHOO! and the
YAHOO! logo are trademarks of Yahoo! Inc.

Therefore, it's important to look beyond the normal benchmarks
such as the Dow when you are building your portfolio. Just because
the entire market is down, doesn't mean every sector is suffering. Or
when the entire market is rallying, there may be some sectors that are
outperforming others. With the amount of pessimism that we've seen
in the market, and with financial leaders around the globe coordinat-
ing bailout and rescue efforts I think the surprise will be on the upside.
Once the bear retreats the emerging bull in whatever sector our analysis suggests will most likely perform better than conventional expectation. Therefore, be nimble, be flexible, and keep your eyes on the data.

Chapter 9

Nimble and Aware

Focusing on the Big Picture

A s an investor, you probably have a long-term time horizon: five years, ten years, or longer. You understand that on any given day or week the market may be up or down. You don't base your long-term investment decisions on where the Dow is today or the Nasdaq is tomorrow. Rather, you're committed to be in the market for the long-term, knowing that—over time—stocks do appreciate in value, even taking into consideration steep corrections such as we've seen in 2008.

Having a long-term view and the discipline to stay the course is commendable. However, a multiyear time horizon for your investment portfolio doesn't mean buy, hold, and forget about it. You need to be actively engaged as an investor. That means staying nimble and alert, with an eye on the big picture.

Granted, the big picture does not change frequently. An economy that is expanding now is likely to keep expanding next month and probably next quarter and the one after that. But that doesn't mean you should let several months or quarters go by without paying attention, not only to the overall trend, but also to the trends within particular sectors. As an investor using ETFs, you can tailor your long-term approach with shorter-term moves to gain exposure to particular industry groups or indices. For example, you can invest in sectors that are expanding, and scale back your exposure to those that are contracting. To do that you need to focus on economics.

Admittedly, my "big picture" approach to investing differs from those strategies that focus only on the market. Some market strategists will look at a stock's price-to-earnings (P/E) ratio to determine if it's a bargain or if it's expensive, or they evaluate whether a stock is trading above or below a specific trend line or moving average of previous prices. As I've stated previously, I'm not the guy to tell you why a stock is cheap at $28 and expensive at $35.

My approach brings together economics and investment with logic, which appeals to my way of thinking. With economics the goal is to find the rationale behind *why* stock prices are moving. For me, it's all about the logic—not trying to predict a particular price target. My perspective is fundamental, based on what I see happening in the economy right now, as well as within certain sectors. As an investment manager, my goal is to identify opportunities where we can ride the wave in the broader market and/or within a particular industry segment when it is doing well. Then when the indications are that the ride has come to an end, I exit the opportunity and move on to the next one.

To do this most effectively, as explained in Chapter 8, I use ETFs, which provide market exposure any way that I care to slice and dice it: from the broad S&P 500 to narrower industry segments such as biotech or healthcare. Whatever I see happening on the economic front, I can find a vehicle to execute my strategy within the ETF universe.

In order to understand the economic picture, I look to the fundamental data. Employment, to me, is always a major indicator. In simplest terms, when jobs are being added, the economy is expanding; when job losses mount, the economy is contracting. This same principle applies within certain segments, all of which is visible in the employment report (as discussed following).

Other indicators that I watch closely are GDP, which measures the output of the overall economy, and investment money flows/stock price momentum.

It's important to understand that one point of data cannot be the basis of a decision. Rather, I'm looking for a trend as the economy and specific sectors go through the cycles of expansion, peak, contraction, and trough over a period of several months. Now I've been doing this for 20 years or so; therefore, I have a database in my head of economic trends. While you may not have the same body of knowledge, you don't need to know off the top of your head how high inflation reached in the 1980s or how low the Fed Funds rate dipped during the Greenspan years. You can develop a working knowledge by watching the economy and key indicators month to month, quarter to quarter.

The Economy is Not the Stock Market

Let's start with a few ground rules. The first rule, or should I say mantra, is that the economy and the stock market are two separate things. The economy is all the output, production, goods, and services bought and sold, imported and exported. It's all the people who are employed, unemployed, getting jobs, and losing jobs. It's consumers buying and businesses selling. All of it, as it's happening right now. The stock market is a mechanism that allows companies to access capital from investors. Now it's true that economic conditions do influence the stock market, and that the stock market can be an advance indicator of economic conditions. But they are not the same thing. You can't look at the stock market on a day when it might be down, say, 100 points in the Dow Jones Industrial Average and declare that the economy is also down. Even on September 29, 2008—the day the Dow dropped an unprecedented 777 points, losing roughly 7 percent of its value—you could not declare based on that stock market data alone that the economy had fallen off a cliff.

If you want to view the economy, you have to look at those things that measure its pulse. The GDP reveals economic output. Employment shows where jobs are being added or cut. While economic reports can fluctuate month-to-month and quarter-to-quarter, as you begin to pay attention, you will see the patterns of expansion and contractions. (And if you want to get a tutorial or a second opinion for what you're looking at, you can always go to our web site, www.etfport.com, for free commentary.)

A Snapshot of the Economy

Looking at the economy real-time can be challenging. It's much easier to look at the data after the fact. For example, you can look at an historic chart and see two or three quarters of declines in GDP and know that was where the economy was slowing down. While that may be a good exercise as you become more familiar with economic reports, it won't help you make investment decisions for today.

Your job is to determine how the economy is performing now by using the available data. In addition to our "big three" of economic reports—GDP, employment, and investment money flows/stock price momentum—there is also a wealth of other data, from the Case-Schiller Home Price Index to minutes from the most recent Federal Open Market Committee (FOMC) report. Rather than risk data overload, let's start with the big three, which over time will provide you with a working knowledge of the economy as it is, right now.

GDP: Measuring Economic Health

Although GDP is a lagging indicator and is often revised after the fact, it is one of the most important gauges of the economy. The GDP reflects the sum of consumption, investment, government spending, and exports, minus imports. Of these components the largest is consumption, accounting for about two-thirds of the total—reflecting the all-important consumer spending.

The GDP data are compiled quarterly, but the report is released monthly. First comes the "advance" report, giving the first look at production and output for the previous quarter. For example, in January the "advance" GDP report for the fourth quarter of the prior year is released. The following month (in this case, February), the "preliminary"

GDP report for the quarter is issued, followed by the "final" GDP report in the subsequent month (March).

Starting with the "advance" report—which is the first look at GDP for the previous quarter—several questions should be considered. The first is, based on the number, how is the economy performing compared with the previous quarter? For example, in July 2008, the advance GDP report for the second quarter showed a quarter-to-quarter increase in output of 1.9 percent, according to advance estimates released by the Bureau of Economic Analysis (see its web site for current and past reports at www.bea.gov). This compared with a growth rate in the first quarter of 0.9 percent.

What this indicated on the surface was that the economy was growing at a faster pace than the previous quarter. While growth was below the average of around 3 percent, the fact that the number was up boded well for the economy to hold its own—at least for the time being. Since this was the advance report, however, there was a chance that the number would be revised. In fact, that's exactly what happened the next month when the preliminary report was released.

In August 2008 the preliminary report showed an upward revision in GDP, with the output of goods and services growing at an annual rate of 3.3 percent in the second quarter. This number was seen as important for two reasons: first, it confirmed that the economy was growing quarter-to-quarter, and second, the rate that was stronger than first estimated in the advance report.

However, revisions in the GDP report are common. At this point the second quarter number had already been revised upward—in this case significantly from the advance to the preliminary report. When the final report came out in September 2008, based on more complete sources of data, we were looking to see if that upward revision of 3.3 percent was confirmed, if it was raised even further, or if it was scaled back.

In the final report, the GDP growth rate on an annual basis was dropped back to 2.8 percent. While the number had been trimmed from 3.3 percent in the preliminary report, it was still up considerably from the advance reading of 1.9 percent. And it showed a healthy gain from the first quarter's relatively slow pace of 0.9 percent. After three GDP reports for the second quarter—advance, preliminary, and final—you could conclude that the economy had grown, and at a pace that was just slightly below the average.

Your next questions would be where and how had the economy grown. (Actually, you would have looked at this data in every month, but for simplicity's sake let's take a look at it in-depth in the final report.) The GDP report always provides explanations as to where expansion and contraction is occurring. For example, was the growth due to an increase in a particular sector? Or were companies building inventories that may help production in the near-term, but presage a possible slowdown in output later on if those inventories don't decrease with consumer and end-user purchases?

In the final report for Q2 2008, the BEA stated: "The increase in real GDP in the second quarter primarily reflected positive contributions from exports, personal consumption expenditures (PCE), nonresidential structures, federal government spending, and state and local government spending that were partly offset by negative contributions from private inventory investment, residential fixed investment, and equipment and software. Imports, which are a subtraction in the calculation of GDP, decreased."

Let's take that step by step. On the plus side, helping the economy to expand were exports (obviously benefiting from a weak dollar at the time), PCE (which is household expenditures on durable and nondurable goods), nonresidential structures, federal government spending, and state and local government spending. On the other side, curtailing growth, were private inventory investment, which meant that inventories were not being built up—causing a drag on the GDP number in that quarter. (Note: If growth is higher in a quarter but inventories were built up, then you might see a decline in the next quarter as inventories are worked off.) Also on the negative column were residential fixed investment, and equipment and software.

Another positive in terms of the GDP number was a drop in imports since these foreign-made goods presumably curtail demand for products manufactured here. The import number can be skewed, however, by the fact that it subtracts parts and components made by U.S.-owned multinationals overseas and imported into the country for final fabrication and finishing. Since the numbers are calculated the same way every month, the result is an index of an expanding or contracting economy.

Based on the data that you've collected and analyzed, what is your conclusion about the health of the economy in the second quarter of 2008? Output was at a stronger pace than in the first quarter, indicating that the U.S. economy had not slowed. While that's not enough data to predict a change in the economic climate or to declare, for example, that the United States would escape a recession, you could make the assumption that the country was not in a recession yet.

Looking ahead to the third-quarter numbers, you'd be looking for the comparison with the second quarter and the first. Did the third quarter GDP number show an acceleration from the second quarter (meaning higher than 2.8 percent), or had the growth in output slowed (coming in at less than 2.8 percent)? As you look at GDP quarter-to-quarter you can build a base of knowledge that tells you much about the overall health of the economy based on the output of goods and services.

Occasionally, GDP "goes negative." For third quarter 2008, GDP came in at −0.5 percent. Obviously that doesn't mean industrial production plants kicked into reverse and factories "unmade" goods. Rather, the rate of production had declined in the most recent period from the previous quarter. A negative GDP reading is a sure sign of a contracting economy. By classic definition, a recession occurs when there are two sequential negative GDP quarterly numbers. Increasing unemployment and declining stock prices, which can be just as painful as a classic recession, also characterize economic contractions.

Another insight that can be gleaned from the GDP report is the level of inventories. Inventories are not part of the GDP equation since goods in the warehouse today were previously counted as output. Nonetheless, the report does make note of inventory levels, which can influence the interpretation of a GDP number. For example, a strong GDP output number won't look as positive if growth in output resulted in higher inventories instead of increased consumer/end user sales. Further, when inventories decline because consumption has increased, it's a sign that economic activity may be picking up soon.

Employment

Employment makes a strong impact as an economic implication, both fundamentally and psychologically. Fundamentally, the job numbers don't lie. Either people are working or they're not. Many economists disagree on how to count those who are working and put more emphasis on the household survey report. Others, such as myself, rely on the Non-Farm Payrolls report, which some claim misses those who are self-employed (they are off the radar, so to speak). The unemployment rate also has its challenges, as it does not count those who have given up looking for work from month-to-month, impacting the percent rating. However, each report if used consistently can be a reliable index of the state of employment. In some cases, one of the reports may give a more accurate picture than the other, but over the entire cycle following employment trends will be one of the most effective ways to get a read on the economy.

Psychologically, the employment report impacts such things as consumer spending. If there is a notable increase in the number of people who are out of work, one would expect that consumer spending will trend lower. Even for those consumers who are still working, increases in the unemployment rate may make them fearful for their own employment situation—and therefore less likely to spend money on big-ticket purchases. This, in turn, will have an impact on the economy, since consumer spending accounts for two-thirds of GDP. Fears of joblessness can also hurt investor sentiment.

Employment is also a direct reflection of the business cycle. In a contracting economy, growth in demand slows and inventories build. Companies cut back production and lay off workers. This helps companies to reduce their labor costs, become more efficient, and improve profitability. During a recession, worker productivity (output per employee) typically improves. As the economy recovers and demand picks up, companies can benefit from lower labor costs for a time. Eventually, however, demand will reach the point at which production must be expanded and additional workers hired. Initially, productivity will decline. However, expansion in payrolls signals that economic recovery is under way.

All of this can be seen in the "Employment Situation Report" (commonly called the unemployment report), which is released the first Friday of every month with data for the previous month. In September 2008, for example, the report showed the unemployment rate rose to 6.1 percent in August from 5.7 percent the month before.

The report also provided a summary of where jobs had been added or lost. Employment fell in manufacturing and employment services, while mining and health care continued to add jobs.

Digging into the report, you can see the magnitude of the job increases and decreases. As explained previously, when you see a sustained growth in job creation in a particular sector, that means it is expanding. Expansion indicates an investment opportunity, which you can capture using an ETF correlated to that sector or industry group. (You can search for information about sector-specific ETFs on the Internet, including at www.etfport.com.)

As you examine the job report month to month, one phenomenon to be aware of is the productivity that results from an economic contraction, and the degree to which the benefits linger. Let's say that a company has 100 workers with an output of 100 units a day. In a contracting economy, demand declines. The company lays off workers because it needs fewer people making less output. In this case, 75 workers are making 75 units a day. When demand picks up, the company doesn't immediately begin hiring more people. At first, those 75 workers will be more productive, perhaps because of a streamlined process or a new technology tool. Now those 75 workers are making 85 units a day. At some point, when demand keeps increasing, the company will begin hiring in order to boost production further, to 95, 100, 110 units, and so on. Production may eventually get to the point where output is 150 units, but it's being produced by 100 workers. That's a significant productivity improvement from the days when it took 100 workers to make 100 units. This is an example of how contractions, while painful, are beneficial in the long run. Companies get more efficient and are able to become healthier and more productive.

Investment Money Flows and Stock Price Momentum

As an indicator, money flows reflect the underlying belief of how well the economy is performing. Good economic growth and a positive employment picture lead to optimism among investors. Secure about their jobs and about employment in general, investors are more likely to invest their money in the market. This makes the stock market one of the most important indicators of economic activity, reflecting both the outlook for growth in corporate output and profitability and the mood of investors.

When analyzing the stock market what we look for is the relative change in stock prices—particularly when looking at the broader market. That's why we focus on the *direction* of money flows/stock price moment. To our way of thinking, it's far more important to know if additional investor money is going into equities and increasing the value of the stock market, as reflected in the major indices such as the Dow, the S&P 500, or the Nasdaq. Or, are investors pulling out of equities, causing stock prices to decline? In some instances, the stock market's behavior may be more telling than the economic data, particularly when the economy is perceived to be at or near a turning point in the trend.

When studying economic data or stock market performance, it's important to look beyond just a single report or a one-month time frame. Trends are developed over time, and it often takes several months for a new trend to be identified and confirmed. With a longer-term perspective, the goal is to look for a consensus among the indicators, not only to confirm the trend but also to gauge its strength. For example, when economic indicators show strong growth and the stock market is showing positive upward momentum, the conditions favor a sustained economic expansion. Conversely, when economic indicators worsen and the stock market turns downward, the stage is set for a sustained contraction.

No Need to be a Passive Investor

If this brief overview of economic data looks like a lot of work, consider this: Aren't you regularly tuned into financial news whether online, in the newspaper, or on television? This is just one more data source, and one you access easily. The schedule of economic reports can be found online. One place to look is that National Bureau of Economic Research (http://www.nber.org/releases/). When the data is released, you can easily go to the web site where the report is posted (for example, BEA's www.bea.gov for the GDP report) and read it for yourself. Yes, you can get the headline and the spin from others (and we certainly invite you to read our interpretation for free at www.etfport. com.), but there is no substitution for doing a little of your own homework. You may very well feel both better informed and empowered.

There is a wealth of economic data to be mined, not only the "big three" of GDP, employment, and money flows, but also consumer sentiment, producer and consumer price index, regional economic data (e.g., Chicago Business Barometer), and Federal Reserve reports. The more informed you are, the more confident you can become in your investment decisions.

Then, using ETFs you will be able to put your knowledge into action. Let's say that over the past three quarters you've noticed a steady increase in GDP: with output growing from a very slow rate of 0.5 percent, to 1.9 percent, and then 3.1 percent. Reading the reports, you notice that inventories are lower, which means that the increased output is going to consumption. In fact, GDP should continue to rise in order to meet demand and fill low inventories. In addition, over the past few months, the unemployment rate has steadily declined, from around 6 percent to near 5 percent. Your sentiment is definitely more bullish as you've seen evidence of an expanding economy. You're not alone: money flows are showing that investors are putting more money into stocks.

Now you can participate in the market in the way that you want. If you think that the broad market is expanding, you can buy ETFs that provide exposure to indexes such as the S&P 500 or the Dow. If you've read that small companies are adding jobs, then you might want to buy the Russell 2000.

As you track GDP and employment, you may notice a particular sector looks hot: perhaps technology or financials. Whatever the sector, there's an ETF to match it. The bottom line is there is no need to be a passive investor anymore, spreading your money around in a half-dozen or more mutual funds. While the old adage of "diversify, diversify" looks good when the market is climbing—and strong growth in one area helps to make up for slower growth or a decline in others— when the market is in a severe contraction as we saw in fall 2008, there is nowhere to hide. Everything is under pressure. As an active investor, you can be in the market when economic conditions are the most favorable and on the sidelines during a contraction. Or, during times of uncertainty, you can scale back your exposure.

And since there is always a bull inside the bear, you can pick those sectors that are growing, even when the rest of the economy is slowing or stalled. Once again, using ETFs, you have a simple and effective way of gaining industry-specific or sector-specific exposure without trying to pick stocks.

Right Sector, Wrong Stock

As I've stated, but it bears repeating, stock picking is a tricky endeavor. You can be right about the direction of the market and about a particular sector, but you can pick the wrong stock. Certain company-specific variables, or maybe a business line in another industry, can weigh on the stock price. Just because a name is familiar doesn't make it a good candidate.

Here's an example of two stocks in the banking sector. Northern Trust made a 52-week high in August 2008 at over $88 a share, at a time when much of the financial sector was under pressure because of the credit crisis. When I looked at the stock's performance, however, I saw that the 52-week high, while an impressive move in the short-term, was actually not that far above where it had been several years before. In September 2000, Northern Trust shares were trading at over $80. In the midst of the eight-year period, the stock had dropped below $30.

Bank of America, meanwhile, was trading at $35 a share. Over that same eight-year period, the stock had risen from the high teens. An impressive move, right? However, at $35 the stock was below recent levels of over $45 a share, which was where Bank of America shares traded from mid-2006 through much of 2007.

Two stocks, two different stories. Northern Trust had returned to its high after being discounted a few years ago when it was seen as being too conservative compared to other financial stocks. That conservatism, which leads to a healthier balance sheet, was being rewarded. Bank of America, meanwhile, was above where it was eight years ago, but had been significantly higher a few years ago when banks were rewarded for taking more risks.

In a perfect world, you would have bought Bank of America in 2000 when it was trading around $18 a share and held it all the way until 2006 to 2007, and sold it for a nice profit at $45. You would have bought Northern Trust when it was at $30 a share and you'd have taken it to its 52-week high at $88 in August 2008. Easier to see in the rear-view mirror than to accomplish in real time.

Using an economic-based approach, you would have been using GDP and the employment report to gauge the health of the economy, as well as money flow information. When you saw the relative strength in the financial sector in the mid-2000s—as jobs were added and money flows were favoring this segment—you would have gotten on board. Rather than choosing one stock, you would have gained exposure to the entire index using an ETF, such as the "XLF." By buying the whole sector you can avoid a problem that's fairly common in investing: buying the wrong stock and missing out on the right one that ends up being the "home run." With a sector approach using an ETF, you have exposure to the blend of the two—along with several other stocks as well. The result is lower risk and lower volatility thanks to an ETF that comprises dozens of stocks, and in some cases hundreds of them. Using a sector approach you would have been able to benefit from the expansion in the financials without the challenge of selecting the best performing stock and then jumping out of that stock and picking up the next company that was taking the sector to the next level. No home run but no strike out either.

The same data that got you into a position in the financial sector would also get you out. When the employment numbers for the sector began to shrink and money flows indicated a turn in investor sentiment—let alone news headlines that trumpeted the credit crisis—you would have exited the financial sector position.

Taking Profits

The statistics show that, over a very long time horizon, buy and hold will work. In fact, not selling is often the most productive thing you can do. The caution there, however, is that you will likely undergo some painful contractions, which are unnecessary. If you are nimble and aware and follow even the most basic of economic data, you will be more likely to get in and out of sectors at favorable times.

Just having a profit, however, isn't a reason to sell. Investors who have been burned sometimes sell too early just to book a profit. They buy at $10 and they sell at $20, happy that they've made money this time. Then the stock or ETF goes to $30 and beyond without them being on board. Why did they sell? Because of an arbitrary price target.

This is an important point to grasp because it can dramatically impact your overall long-term performance. By selling at an arbitrary price you are, in fact, making a very specific decision. If that decision over time was profitable, it would make sense to sell at the profit price and buy the stock back at a lower price and book the profit. You would not even need to do the first buy. However, since stocks are positively sloped, and some will go up and some will go down over time, if you sell at the wrong time you limit the amount of money you statistically need to make on that stock. Further, you might end up taking a loss on some stocks that ends up being greater than the profit you've made, which will impact the entire portfolio.

Particularly with ETFs I would rather have a fundamental reason to sell. If a sector is showing slower output in the GDP report and/or is losing jobs, then I'd be more apt to sell than just because I had finally booked a profit. By sticking to the same discipline over time you can enhance your overall portfolio performance rather than picking arbitrary entry and exit points. It will even be more productive to pick a date like month-end or quarter-end and make all investment decisions before that date and execute them on the same schedule each time. Sometimes that will hurt and sometimes that will help, but in the end it will be far better than reacting spontaneously.

The Bull Inside the Bear: Diversification Using ETFs

The buzzwords of "diversify" and "game plan" are, of course, essential, but another word, "correlation," is equally important. The more assets that you hold in your portfolio (diversification) the better it is for you—provided that they are noncorrelating. Otherwise what's the use?

If you buy several assets but they all move in tandem with each other, where is the protection in that?

An ETF diversifies your stock exposure to a sector. The risk of one company is almost eliminated when you purchase an ETF, and you can have the true exposure of the sector. Multiple ETFs diversify you even more, provided the sectors or indexes are noncorrelating. What is the point of having exposure to the Dow 30 and the S&P 500 if they have a .85 correlation? (The closer the correlation is to 1.0 the more alike they are.)

Be nimble but don't make snap decisions. Your investment portfolio is not a day trading account. I can't see the necessity of making more than a few changes in your portfolio each quarter or actually each year. Try to wait for at least two data points before jumping in.

Stocks can go to zero and companies can file for bankruptcy; sectors cannot. This makes it easier to deploy your cash when things look the darkest.

I wouldn't have advised trying to buy Bear Sterns, Wachovia, and Lehman Brothers no matter how cheap their stocks looked at the time. To me they were no better than buying a lottery ticket and probably with about the same odds. However, if the fundamentals suggested dipping a toe into a sector ETF with some confidence then you'd know that a complete loss was not in the cards. And the better the fundamentals behind any sector the greater your chances for a win.

Chapter 10

Thoughts on Life—and Investing

W̶hen I started writing this book early in the second quarter of 2008, the financial news was filled with the bursting of a "housing bubble" and a "credit crunch." As work on the book continued, the terminology escalated to credit crisis and then financial meltdown. What we've witnessed in the second half of 2008 has been perhaps the greatest financial crisis of the past 50 years.

The credit crisis and subsequent financial system meltdown—as well as a stock market crash—have given me a reason to pause and reflect. Not about my firm's investment philosophy or objectives; actually, our clients fared quite well. The tools that we discussed in previous chapters, such as employment trends and other fundamental indicators, at the very least allowed us to reduce exposures and in some cases get out of major equity indices and even get short. After reading the book thus far, I am sure by now you get the picture of how this works.

Assets experience distinct cycles. Cycles are determined by employment trends, and trends are guided (up and down) by changes in behavior, government policies, and Fed actions that impact money growth. If you follow that you should be able to find the bull inside the bear.

While all these lessons are very important, and they guide the decisions that we make every day, there *is* a bigger picture. It's about perception of money and return. It's about cost of capital and cost of labor. And it's about financial objectives and realistic expectations of risk versus return. These are the things worth thinking about at least as much as (or even more than) the present economic trends.

Writing a book on economics, investing, and the stock market during the worst financial crises we have experienced in our lifetime is sort of like planning your honeymoon in Bali during a tsunami and wondering why no one at the reservation desk at the five-star luxury resort is answering the phone. Does it really matter what the travel advice and restaurant recommendations are anymore? Well, truth be told it may not, but the marriage will still go on and hopefully be loving and wonderful regardless.

Don't misunderstand. I am not trying to deflect the current market conditions and get everyone to start singing "Kumbaya" as they reflect on what they do have in life, such as health, family, friends, and so forth. In fact, I get frustrated and annoyed when a bad business environment or bear market is responded to with comments like, "You should appreciate those who love you," or, "Look at your beautiful family," and "Count your blessings; you have your health." I get it that this stuff is very important—and even more important—than the material things. But we do not live in an either/or world. I do, as many of you, appreciate what we have. I have a wonderful wife, Eileen: a super woman who is an attorney, very involved in the community and serves on charity boards, a go-to person with any problem issue or question, who has time for everyone. I appreciate my son, Spencer, who at the age of three-and-a-half is one of the wisest and most caring people I know. I am amazed at his thought processes. And of course I value my extended family and friends—and all the good that is in my life.

But we need to keep life—and our money—in perspective. And since this book is about economics and investment, my purpose is to give you a few thoughts on both (with some life advice thrown in for good measure). Added to the fundamental economics and investment lessons you've already learned in the previous nine chapters, I hope my thoughts will be helpful—and maybe even enlightening.

Worry About the Right Things

While it's good to keep perspective about what's good in life—family, friends, and what makes you happy—it's important to make sure you're making good decisions that will help you live a better life. That means focusing on the right things and not the tangential, fear-based things.

I recall reading an article a few years ago about why we worry about the wrong things. The article went on to state that we make certain decisions with little regard to logic when worrying about our fate, health, or money—particularly during fear or crises. For example, it talked about the SARs outbreaks and anthrax scares, and how people were suddenly trying to buy obscure antibiotics and other hard-to-come-by antidotes. Stories abounded of people bribing their doctors for a stash of medications that they didn't need because of any current health crisis. Rather, they were willing to pay thousands of dollars to have a personal supply—just in case. The truth is that no one in the United States died from either SARS or anthrax. But more to the point, hundreds and thousands of people die each year from the flu when a vaccine is available for about $20, and in some cases is free. Yet only a small percentage of people take that precaution.

Or when an outbreak of mad cow disease is reported, beef consumption drops 20 percent or more—even though not one human fatality has ever been linked to mad cow. However, heart attacks and high cholesterol are a proven link to hundreds of thousand of deaths. Yet that doesn't deter beef consumption.

The examples are limitless, and they transcend examples of our health into the area of financial planning. Investors worry about the safety of their bank deposits even though their account is insured by the Federal Deposit Insurance Corporation. Yet they will buy a stock willy-nilly, even though they have little knowledge of what the firm does, what it makes, or what's on its balance sheet. The likelihood of profitably picking a single stock is less than 50/50, while the likelihood of losing money on a bank deposit is one in a hundred million. Actually, stock investing in general is quite random. Determining the price of say, Microsoft, within $5 is merely a rounding error as the viability of the company is not at all impacted by $5 swings in the stock price. Yet we have opinions on the next $5 move, and will take a risk based on that opinion, versus focusing on something with much higher assurance of the value and direction, such as the overall market.

People will go into survival mode for the crash that doesn't come, but they won't prepare for the more likely event of a recession. You would be so much farther ahead if you would maximize the highly likely events and provide yourself with a bigger cushion for the uncertain and less productive outcomes. I could give countless examples of worrying about events that have a much smaller probability of occurrence, but garnered greater emphasis by investors and the general population. The point is that if we can learn to look at each event and evaluate it on its merits or lack thereof we can make better decisions that are more productive to our well-being and to achieving our goals.

The Credit-Based Economy

Here is the next point to consider. Why do people work? If you said, "To make money," I'll ask you to reconsider in a moment.

Here's another question that's even more difficult to contemplate: What is the cost of working eight hours a day at a job you love compared to the one that pays the most? That is the hardest thing to measure in economics: utility or marginal utility. It impacts on employment the most, and since employment is a large driver of our economy and my investment philosophy, this is a very important statistic to try to measure.

Let's return to the first point for a moment, the notion of working for money. Money actually has no value as we are on a fiat monetary system. Therefore, the only value money has is the goods and services for which you can exchange it. Perhaps there is some intrinsic value in just knowing you have money and getting more. Many people aspire to accumulate money, and that's a good thing as it motivates a for-profit attitude that is needed to efficiently function as a society and economy.

What has changed over the past few decades is the rise of the goods and services economy/society. Consumer spending now makes up over 70 percent of GDP and—here we go, drum roll please—consumer spending is done about half on credit. (With younger consumers, the percentage of spending with credit cards is over 50 percent, while older consumers use credit cards under half the time.) This clearly shows that we no longer exchange money for goods and services; we use credit.

Actually, we no longer work for money. We work to increase our credit availability. In fact, the economy was able to be regulated by increasing and decreasing credit availabity and the cost of credit. The recession of 2001 to 2002 was one of the only recessions that did *not* see an increase in savings, which ultimately leads to an increase in spending to help usher in the next expansion. Instead, spending was increased by expansion of credit and debt. This, of course, materially impacts the savings rate, because we no longer need to save to consume. Everything is available now. Savings has a positive impact on an economy because this money is generally invested or held at a bank that, in turn, lends it out. This activity helps keep the economy running.

You know the drill. Savings deposited in banks will get loaned out, and you will be paid interest. The loan is generally collateralized by an asset such as a house or real estate or a factory. The loan is used to buy an asset that will appreciate in value or help run a business that generates a profit and hires more workers, who get a paycheck and consume… and the cycle continues. With a credit society, some of the pieces that help smooth and transition from one cycle to another get ignored. At first it seems easy to cure a slowdown or contraction without experiencing any pain by lowering the cost of credit, which gives you a breather. Then, by extending more credit, the ball gets rolling again.

However, nothing was cured on a fundamental basis. Fat was not cut and the problems that caused the contraction are still underlining the economy. It is a proverbial house of cards that appears to have finally fallen. The solutions are really the same as always; however, we need to fix the financial system first. Then we can have a real recession—not like that excuse for a recession we had in 2001 to 2002. We need a recession that cuts fat, cuts debt, reduces payrolls, and increases savings. From that we will get productivity gains that ultimately translate into profits and employment gains. Then the cycle can start all over again.

One of the positive outcomes of the recession would be for people to kick their deadly credit addiction—not because they've gone to rehab, but because there is no more "booze." With credit becoming harder to come by and more expensive, people will have to wean themselves off it. That will be so much healthier for them, and for the economy, in the long run.

While consumers did get somewhat out of hand—spending a little more on the house, running up the credit-card balances, and so forth—Wall Street and Corporate America were really on a binge as they became highly overleveraged. The deleveraging of the system, which is happening as of this writing, may be painful, but it is absolutely necessary.

What you as a consumer should take away from this process is the need to take a more realistic view of your own financial situation. How much debt can you comfortably bear? And what are you doing to save for your future? These are timeless questions, but the time to really contemplate them is now.

Don't Fight the Cycles

If you haven't guessed already by reading this book let me tell it to you plainly: I'm big into cycles. I think cycles are important to recognize in the economy and the markets—and in life. Recognizing cycles allows you to be better prepared and to be constantly aware of the next cycle, whether positive or negative. When the markets contract, they will recover. The same holds with life as well. And with each cycle you take something away that helps in the next cycle and each full turn moves up the curve, so that the trough of the next cycle will be higher than the peak of the last.

Getting back to the economy and the cycles, I like to think of the board game Monopoly. It is a loose metaphor for an economy and society where everyone starts out with the same "chance" to own Boardwalk and Park Place and reach a level of comfort. However, in the game Monopoly there is only one winner. The rules are set at the beginning of the game and we all play until someone controls everything. Players accumulate property, build homes and hotels, pay taxes, and collect rents. Sound familiar? At the end of some period of time—and usually after anguish for one of the players who has mortgaged everything, hoping for one more spin around the board—one of the players owns most of everything.

Now I ask the question, what if another player existed? Let's call him Uncle Sam. And the rules were a bit different for Uncle Sam. He could add a tax or decrease a tax; he could not let you build a hotel on Park Place, or require fees and licenses that might make your decision to buy an asset or utility less desirable. What if this new player, Uncle Sam, could reach into the box and take Monopoly money to distribute to everyone in order to even out the game whenever it gets out of balance? Could these powers allow the game to go on indefinitely?

Viewing the system as one big Monopoly game, we have to wonder how the game affects all the others—including the ones playing by a different set of rules at another table. Could it be that our version of the game—with a democratic/capitalistic society and an Uncle Sam to help things along—will eventually influence those other games as well? Taking the metaphorical into the rhetorical, will the influx of capitalism into a place like China begin to influence the system from the inside, from a Communist state into one that may be somewhat more democratic? That may never happen, but even slight movements can be monumental. As George Soros observed about the marketplace, we may never get to equilibrium, but approaching it is beneficial.

In the end, it may be the cycles that determine how the game is played and by whom, as economies strengthen and weaken. We can only play—and observe what happens.

Be Discerning

While much of what I've written thus far sounds very philosophical, I do want to add some practicality as well, which I hope will help you to make better decisions. We live in a society that likes to find someone or something to blame; where sound bites sell and knee-jerk reactions are made for better or usually for worse.

There have been numerous examples of the "instant analysis" on topics such as taxes, short selling, and blaming the speculator or the hedge fund manager. We like to say "this is good" and "that is bad"—clear cut and definitive. But the world is far too complicated for that type of thinking. We need to take a deeper and more discerning look into how things work. Then you can make up your own mind about how to view things. And if you reach the conclusion that things are more complex than they first appear, then know you are in good company.

The Economy and Politics

I am often asked which party is better for the economy and the stock market. Aren't Republican policies more pro-business? (Or so many people think.) The nonpartisan truth is that the policies of both the Republicans and the Democrats are bad for the economy and business. That's a simple fact. However, sometimes one party's policies are better than the other's for the *current* environment.

Let's look at taxes. It appears we all dislike paying more taxes; that seems quite clear. But what if we looked at the bigger picture of a person's entire financial condition, of which taxes were one component. Now, let's say you paid $1,000 more in taxes, but because of that your business increased 20 percent, the stock market appreciated 15 percent, and the interest rate on your mortgage and other debt declined. Wouldn't you pay an extra $1,000?

Now, what if you received a $1,000 tax refund, but your financial condition deteriorated by $5,000 because of a decline in business conditions and the stock market? Would you take it?

I am *not* saying that is the case, or that higher taxes are good. (And please read that last sentence a second time so you understand me.) Rather, I want to illustrate the point that sometimes higher taxes produce greater overall benefits, and sometimes they are just higher taxes. If it's just higher taxes then your financial health declines by the amount of the additional levy. Worse yet, maybe the higher tax will somehow translate into an incentive for the wrong behavior and result in an even bigger loss than the amount of tax paid (which lately seems to be the more likely outcome).

The goal is to produce economically positive results and create jobs and efficiencies. I admit that taxes don't usually do that, but sometimes the unseen benefits go unnoticed. Once again, it's a case of needing to be discerning about what is "good" and what is "bad," and what's to blame.

The Blame Game

If we always look to place blame, we won't fix the system or the problem. For example, high energy prices plagued the economy during 2007 and the first half of 2008. In the energy market, blame was placed on the speculator, the trader, and the hedge fund manager. No one thought to blame the consumer for reckless consumption habits or the explosive growth of the ex-burbs that require greater energy usage, or low energy-efficiency vehicles, or even rapid population growth.

No, the blame was put squarely on the speculator. For some reason the speculators or traders were thought to be able to cause the problem—supposedly buying because they "knew" prices would go up. So they bought and their actions caused the price to go higher. Please! If that were the case, with very little barrier to entry, why wouldn't everyone do that? Why wouldn't airlines speculate in the energy market and reap huge profits when oil soared past $120 per barrel?

The thinking was that speculators really were the ones who drove prices of something that's needed (such as crude oil) to artificially high levels. The speculator has the power to acquire and then, because there is no other supply available except what the speculator has purchased, everyone else is forced to buy at an inflated price. Even if this scenario occurred, higher prices would result in reduced demand or alternatives being created, even for the most inelastic of things. Further, as prices moved to levels considered to be too high, those same speculators would start selling to book their profits and would even increase their selling to take short positions. And so the market would return to equilibrium.

Without the speculator, it's possible that the pent-up demand for goods wouldn't have decreased. Further, the role of the speculator is needed in both directions. Otherwise, the only one with any power in the marketplace is the producer who controls supply, which is a much unhealthier scenario than some speculative activity.

Statistics about the futures market, which is one of the most common ways to speculate in markets such as oil, gold, and other commodities, show that *90 percent of speculators lose money*. Here's one reason why: higher prices will eventually lead to increased supply or decreased demand, both of which will eventually push prices lower. And when that change happens, the speculators are the ones who get hurt. Those who bought thinking prices were going higher have to sell on the way down—and as prices plummet their selling increases. Even the Hunt brothers, who were infamously accused of cornering the silver market, lost billions. Speculation has a limited profit potential.

The role of the speculator, however, is important to the market. Speculators create efficiencies and help prices reach their equilibrium.

The ban on short-selling proved this. When speculative activity was curbed, the market became more erratic and less efficient. The short-selling ban was put on stocks that were not in good shape. For example, some banks (which may have been on the Federal Reserve's watch list) could no longer be "shorted." Short-sellers had to cover with buying activity that artificially pushed up stocks, some of which reached 52-week highs. The bid/offer spread got wider because of a lack of liquidity in the market. As the short-selling speculator got out of the market, Joe Retail saw stock prices go higher and decided to get in—at artificially elevated prices.

And later when the market went down because of a lack of buying, it became highly erratic. Joe Retail got burned and began dumping the portfolio. Selling was indiscriminate because of panic.

Short-sellers aren't always right, but they are not the problem. And the volume of short-selling activity is small compared to the overall mix. Banning the short-seller is not the solution. Letting the market operate more freely is better for all involved.

While the government restricted short selling in certain equities and many Congressman and Senators attacked or verbally ridiculed speculation in the energy market, everyone needs to be careful when it comes to painting things as "good" and "bad" without understanding how the marketplace works. What about speculation that helps bring down interest rates at a time when companies need to lower their borrowing costs? What about the speculator who is willing to buy the less-than-Triple-A-rated corporate bond, which the average investor won't touch?

Speculators equal liquidity, which is the lifeblood of the market, at least in my book (no pun intended). As a discerning individual you need to make up your own mind.

The Bull Inside the Bear—Is *You*

If I can say this one more time, allow me to repeat myself: It is all about cycles. Markets, assets, and life all seem to experience some sort of order that keeps occurring with some pattern. While it is difficult and maybe even impossible to forecast when the cycle will change, it is certainly possible to identify the cycle we are in currently.

Whether you personally are in a growth period or a rebuilding stage, if it appears that all is lost never fear; the next expansion is around the corner. Maybe you cannot see it, and perhaps it feels like things will never get better, but rest assured your emergency rate cut may be just around the corner.

The more educated and empowered you are, the better decisions you will make—not by listening to the talking heads on television or reading the latest blog posting. You will do your own homework and your own research, paying attention to the economic indicators that tell you what's happening. This is not difficult, and it will put you in the driver's seat as you make investment decisions based on better rationale than buy-hold-and-forget it or panicking and following the crowd.

You will have your eyes open and your mind clear to spot the next bull as it arises from inside the bear.

Notes

Chapter 1: How Has the World Changed?

1. *The Wall Street Journal*, Review and Outlook, "The End of Wall Street," September 23, 2008, http://online.wsj.com/article/SB122212648830465179 .html.

2. CNBC.com, "Warren Buffett to CNBC: U.S. Economy in Recession by 'Common Sense Definition,'" March 3, 2008, http://www.cnbc .com/id/23446988.

Chapter 2: Bubbles, Bursts, and Blips: A View of the Past

1. History.com, "FRD Takes United States off Gold Standard," http://www.history .com/this-day-in-history.do?action=VideoArticle&id=59256.

2. Time.com, "Shrinking Role for U.S. Money," October 15, 1979, http:// www.time.com/time/magazine/article/0,9171,916948-1,00.html.

3. Federal Deposit Insurance Corporation, "The S&L Crisis: A Chrono-Bibliography," http://www.fdic.gov/bank/historical/s&l/.

4. Bureau of Economic Analysis, "Table C. Historical Measures," June 2008, http://www.bea.gov/scb/pdf/2008/06%20June/D-Pages/0608dpg_c.pdf.

5. Federal Reserve, "Remarks by Chairman Alan Greenspan at the Annual Dinner and Francis Boyer Lecture of The American Enterprise Institute for

Public Policy Research, Washington, D.C.," December 5, 1996, http://www
.federalreserve.gov/boarddocs/speeches/1996/19961205.htm.

Chapter 3: Inflation: The Factor That Is Always with Us

1. Bureau of Labor Statistics, "The Effect of Outsourcing and Offshoring on
   BLS Productivity Measures," March 26, 2004, http://www.bls.gov/lpc/lproff-
   shoring.pdf.

2. Douglas R. LeRoy, "Scheduled wage increases and cost-of-living provisions
   in 1981," Monthly Labor Review, Bureau of Labor Statistics, January 1981,
   http://www.bls.gov/opub/mlr/1981/01/art2full.pdf.

3. PBS.org, "Commanding Heights: Paul Volcker," September 26, 2000, http://
   www.pbs.org/wgbh/commandingheights/shared/minitextlo/int_paulvol-
   cker.html#4.

4. FederalReserve.gov, Remarks by Chairman Alan Greenspan, "Monetary
   Policy Twenty-Five Years after October 1979," October 7, 2004, http://www
   .federalreserve.gov/boarddocs/speeches/2004/200410073/default.htm.

5. FederalReserve.gov, Testimony of Chairman Alan Greenspan, "The Federal
   Reserve's Semiannual Monetary Policy Report," February 26, 1997, http://
   www.federalreserve.gov/boarddocs/hh/1997/february/testimony.htm.

6. FederalReserve.gov, Testimony of Chairman Alan Greenspan, "Federal Reserve
   Board's Semiannual Monetary Policy Report to the Congress," July 15, 2003,
   http://www.federalreserve.gov/boarddocs/hh/2003/july/testimony.htm.

7. FederalReserve.gov, Chairman Ben S. Bernanke, "Semiannual Monetary
   Policy Report to the Congress," July 15, 2008, http://www.federalreserve
   .gov/newsevents/testimony/bernanke20080715a.htm.

Chapter 4: The Credit Cycle

1. Office of Federal Housing Enterprise Oversight, 2008 Report to Congress,
   http://www.ofheo.gov/media/annualreports/ReporttoCongress2008.pdf.

2. John Cassidy, "The Minsky Moment," The New Yorker, February 4, 2008,
   http://www.newyorker.com/talk/comment/2008/02/04/080204taco_talk_
   cassidy?printable.

Chapter 5: The Housing Bubble: From Watch to Warning

1. WhiteHouse.gov, "President Reiterates Goal on Homeownership," June 18,
   2002, http://www.whitehouse.gov/news/releases/2002/06/20020618-1.html.

2. U.S. Census Bureau, "Census Bureau Reports on Residential Vacancies and
   Home Ownership," April 28, 2008, http://www.census.gov/hhes/www/
   housing/hvs/qtr108/q108press.pdf.

3. U.S. Census Bureau, "Net Worth and the Assets of Households: 2002," April 2008, http://www.census.gov/prod/2008pubs/p70-115.pdf.

4. FederalReserve.gov, "Testimony of Alan Greenspan, Monetary Policy and the Economic Outlook," Before the Joint Economic Committee, U.S. Congress, April 17, 2002 http://www.federalreserve.gov/boarddocs/testimony/2002/20020417/default.htm

5. Ruth Simon and James R. Hagerty, "Mortgage Defaults Spread, Snagging More Borrowers," *The Wall Street Journal,* March 2, 2007, http://www.realestatejournal.com/buysell/mortgages/20070302-simon.html.

6. FederalReserve.gov, "Remarks by Chairman Alan Greenspan: The Mortgage Market and Consumer Debt," October 19, 2004, http://www.federalreserve.gov/boarddocs/speeches/2004/20041019/default.htm.

7. Congressional Budget Office, "Housing Wealth and Consumer Spending," January 2007, http://www.cbo.gov/ftpdocs/77xx/doc7719/01-05-Housing.pdf.

Chapter 6: The Fed as FEMA

1. FederalReserve.gov, "Brief History of the 1987 Stock Market Crash with a Discussion of the Federal Reserve Response," Mark Carlson, November 2006, http://www.federalreserve.gov/pubs/feds/2007/200713/.

2. FederalReserve.gov, "Testimony of Chairman Alan Greenspan, Private-sector Refinancing of the Large Hedge Fund, Long-Term Capital Management," October 1, 1998, http://www.federalreserve.gov/boarddocs/testimony/1998/19981001.htm.

3. FederalReserve.gov, "Remarks by Chairman Alan Greenspan, Before the President's Council on Year 2000 Conversion," Financial Sector Group, Year 2000 Summit, September 17, 1999

4. FederalReserve.gov, "Chairman Ben S. Bernanke, Semiannual Monetary Policy Report to the Congress," Before the Committee on Banking, Housing, and Urban Affairs, U.S. Senate, July 15, 2008

5. FederalReserve.gov, "Chairman Ben S. Bernanke, Semiannual Monetary Policy Report to the Congress," July 15, 2008, http://www.federalreserve.gov/newsevents/testimony/bernanke20080715a.htm.

6. FederalReserve.gov, Press Release, September 16, 2008, http://www.federalreserve.gov/newsevents/press/other/20080916a.htm.

About the Author

Robert Stein is an economist, portfolio manager, and senior partner of Astor Asset Management, LLC, in Chicago, which uses a macro-economic model to make investment decisions. He is also the founder of etfport.com, which provides free information to investors on exchange-traded funds. Stein started his career as an analyst at the Federal Reserve. Stein is author of *Inside Greenspan's Briefcase*, published by McGraw Hill in 2002. Stein writes frequently about the markets, and has been featured in the *Wall Street Journal, Business Week,* the *New York Times, USA Today,* and *Reuters,* and can be seen on CNN, CNBC, Fox News, and Bloomberg Television. He is also the vice chairman of the board of advisors of Glenkirk, an organization that serves those with developmental disabilities.

Index